HOW TO

WRITE

A GOOD

ADVERTISEMENT

A Short Course

by VICTOR O. SCHWAB

in Copywriting

HOW TO
WRITE
A GOOD
ADVERTISEMENT

Wilshire Book Company
22647 Ventura Blvd. #314
Woodland Hills, CA 91364

At the very end of many chapters of this book appear reprints of various articles and verses written over the years by Mr. Schwab for *Printer's Ink* and other advertising publications. These (and certain of the material in the body of some of the chapters themselves) are now reprinted with the kind permission of the publications in which they originally appeared.

LIBRARY OF CONGRESS CATALOG CARD NUMBER: 61-10843

ISBN 0-87980-397-5

To my wife,

VILMA NOBLE SCHWAB,

without whose constant and confounded

"I've taken the cover off the typewriter; get going"

I would never have finished writing this book

CONTENTS

Contents ix

PREFACE

This book might well have carried the subtitle *Or 44 Years in the Copy Department* instead of its present one. Even a copywriter, whose breed is not noteworthy for arithmetical prowess, could not escape arriving at the conclusion that the number of years from 1917 to 1961 totals forty-four. And, Heaven help me!, for that seeming aeon of time the major interest of the author has been advertising copy—good, bad, and indifferent.

That a large measure of this past experience has been associated with a particularly demanding kind of advertising copy may, as will be explained, be an advantageous circumstance for the reader of this book, regardless of what type of copywriting job confronts him.

For the subject of the book is *not* the writing of mail-order copy. Its sole purpose is to lend a hand to any copywriter (or student of copywriting) whose ambition is to create advertisements which are more resultful, no matter what the product is or how and where it is sold.

As to why the author's background of experience may represent an advantageous circumstance for such copywriters, I will leave to an infinitely more capable pen than mine—that of no less an authority than Claude G. Hopkins, one of the greatest copywriters of "general" advertising who ever lived: "Mail-order advertising is difficult. But it is educational. It keeps one on his mettle. It fixes one's viewpoint on cost and result. The advertising-writer learns more from mail-order advertising than from any other."

Therefore, if you are looking for guidance specifically concerned with the writing of mail-order advertising, this is not your book. On the other hand, if in the writing of any type of advertising you want more of your copy to achieve the selling effectiveness imperative for any mail-order man who wants to continue eating heartily, this book may prove helpful to you. At any rate, you are the person for whom it was written.

Much of its information will probably recall to your mind the aphorism, "We need not so much to be instructed as to be reminded." And that's all to the good. Finally, and appertaining to the passages which are reminiscent in nature, the author has tried to avoid any necessity for later having to admit, like Mark Twain, that "When I was very young I could remember anything, whether it happened or not. But now I am older and I can only remember the latter."

VICTOR O. SCHWAB

INTRODUCTION

The advertisement itself is the keystone in the arch of sales. Most sales difficulties (for example, problems of dealer distribution, co-operation, and brand switching) actually hark right back to impotent advertisements. They were too easily resistible; simply not good enough to make people see, read, and act upon them: to go out and demand the product advertised and no other.

Poor copy cannot overcome faults or gaps in dealer distribution; it cannot even cash in on the finest dealer setups. But *good* copy can, and does, surmount many dealer difficulties, making them secondary, and selling in spite of them.

Therefore, since either the blame for failure or the credit for success in many sales campaigns can rightly be laid at the doorstep of the advertisements themselves, the first five chapters of this book concentrate upon certain basic elements of a good advertisement. This is essential, because, as Condé Nast once stated, "The more factors we do not know, the more important it is for us to isolate those very few factors which we count on."

What are these fundamentals? Five of them are discussed in our first chapters. They are (1) Get Attention; (2) Show People an Advantage; (3) Prove It; (4) Persuade People to *Grasp* This Advantage; (5) Ask for Action.

Most advertising copywriters know these fundamentals. Many of us practice them. Some of us should get back to them. Whether one is now studying to go into the field of copywriting, whether he is new in the craft, or whether he has been a practitioner in it for years, his knowledge—*and practice*—of these fundamentals will determine the extent of his success. As Daniel Defoe said, "An old and experienced pilot loses a ship by his assurance and over-confidence of his knowledge as effectively as the young pilot does by his ignorance and want of experience."

So this book will strip down to fundamentals, try to forget the furbelows. For, as time goes on, every line of creative work gets cluttered up with impressive jargon and off-the-beam technicalities, with professional palaver that strays far away from the main objective. Someone has said, "Whenever people are particularly muddled in their thinking they invent big words to cover their confusion."

Yet, after all, is advertising itself really such a complicated thing? Its basic purpose is simple: to make people buy a product or a service. Not just to make them pause, or admire, or even merely to believe. For advertising is nothing but an expense (not an investment) unless it gets the kind of action desired by the advertiser.

That's a very clear purpose. But in practice—that's where the fuzziness comes in. And the result: Beautiful examples of the art of advertising are produced, printed, admired—and, page after page, flipped over by the public.

HOW TO

WRITE

A GOOD

ADVERTISEMENT

CHAPTER 1

GET ATTENTION

There are five fundamentals in the writing of a good advertisement:

1. Get Attention
2. Show People an Advantage
3. Prove It
4. Persuade People to *Grasp* This Advantage
5. Ask for Action

An advertisement cannot stimulate sales if it is not read; it cannot be read if it is not seen; and it will not be seen unless it can Get Attention. That's the round robin which Daniel Starch must have had in mind when he wrote "The attention-value of an advertisement is approximately twice as important as the actual convincingness of the test itself."

YOU—THE UNINVITED GUEST

Do not underestimate the fierce competition you face in getting attention. Nobody in the world (except you) is waiting for your advertisement to appear. Everybody in the world (except you) would much rather read the news, comics, stories, articles, editorials or even the obituaries.

You, the advertiser, are the Uninvited Guest—actually, let's face it, an intruder. No reader asked you, or paid you, to join the party which he is having with the publication he has bought. You paid to get in.

The reader has bought the publication for news, entertainment, or instruction which is of helpful personal value. So that is what your advertisement also has to provide—if you are to stand any chance of competing with the publication's editorial matter for the interest of the reader. And then, to make him pay you for your product, you must make it pay him to read about it.

Successful advertisers purposely start from this premise: People don't want to read advertising—not even mine. Then they work their way around this 8-ball by shooting that much harder for advertisements that, as Arthur Brisbane defined good writing, are "easier to read than to skip." They try to offer so enticing a "reward for reading" that people will want to read their advertisements right through —against any competition, editorial or commercial.

TWO OBSTACLES—BEFORE THE CONTEST EVEN BEGINS

Of course, before *your* advertisement even has an opportunity to compete for attention against a publication's editorial matter and the other advertisements in it, there are a few other obstacles which have to be met and overcome.

First, the publication (if delivered by mail to a subscriber) must be unwrapped and at least made ready for reading. Actually, many thousands of copies are not opened, more than at first thought you might imagine. The issues come pretty fast, particularly the weeklies, and many people just "do not get around" to them. That is why advertising men check carefully on the amount of newsstand circulation of a publication. For this represents circulation to people who have actually gone out and purchased single copies, not copies which "come to them" as a result of a subscription ordered previously— perhaps at a cut-price subscription rate so low that the subscriber, having invested so little, can be quite casual about reading them.

Second, the contents of the publication must at least be examined —and the more of the reader's time which the editorial material in the publication attracts, the better chance your advertisement has of being noticed. Here, however, you again lose a certain additional percentage of potential readership: those who, in spite of how much time they may give to the editorial content of the publication, give very little of it (some readers claim none at all!) to the reading of the advertisements in it.

One survey indicates that the average person reads only four advertisements in the average magazine. Another investigator, George B. Hotchkiss, in his *Advertising Copy,* tells us that to read a metropolitan newspaper completely through requires at least fourteen hours—and a study made for the Association of National Advertisers cites a survey demonstrating that "over 66 per cent of a large group of business and professional men spent 15 minutes or less in reading daily newspapers."

Only after these two obstacles have been surmounted can your advertisement face the contest of winning the attention of as many as possible of those who do unwrap the publication, who do examine it with some thoroughness, and who do include the advertisements in their examination or reading. And, to capture that attention, you've got to earn it—either with your headline or with your layout, and preferably with both.

How Important Is the Headline?

How important a part does the headline alone play in the accomplishment of our first purpose: Get Attention? Perhaps you have read somewhere that 50 per cent of the value of an entire advertisement is represented by the headline itself. Or 70 per cent. Or 80 per cent. The truth is that you cannot possibly evaluate it in percentages.

For example, what percentage *better* is an automobile that runs beautifully as compared with one that won't run at all? It's the same with headlines. One can be almost a total failure in accomplishing even its primary purpose: to induce people to *start* reading the body matter (the copy) of the advertisement. Another headline can work almost like magic in enticing readers by the thousands into an ad whose copy moves people to action and thus moves products off the shelves.

Yes, there is really that much difference in the power of headlines. It isn't enough to cram persuasiveness into the body matter. Some of the most tremendous flops among advertisements contain body matter filled with convincing copy. But it just wasn't capsuled into a good headline. And so the excellent copy did not even get a reading.

For, obviously, it is the headline that gets people into the copy; the copy doesn't get them into the headline. In other words, the copywriter's aim in life should be to try to make it harder for people to pass up his advertisement than to read it. And right in his headline he takes the first, and truly giant, step on the road to that goal.

So much for the importance of headlines—and for the staggering waste and loss of effectiveness when expensive advertising space is devoted to displaying poor ones.

THE SOLE PURPOSE OF A HEADLINE

What is the sole purpose of a headline? To make it crystal clear we'll use a simple and sufficiently accurate analogy.

The headline of an advertisement is like a flag being held up by a flagman alongside a railroad track. He is using it to try to get the immediate attention of the engineer of an approaching train—so that he can give him some kind of message. In the case of advertising, on that flag is printed the headline of an advertisement.

Let's carry the analogy further. The train consists of a fast-moving modern Diesel engine and one car. The engineer will (most often) be the mother and/or father of a family. The one dependent car contains the rest of the family. They are all speeding along the track of their daily lives—moving fast in accordance with the hectic tempo of today.

The message on that flag (the headline of the advertisement) must be persuasive. Yes, and persuasive *enough* to compete with all the other distractions of life. It must capture attention. And it must offer a "reward for reading." This reward must be sufficiently attractive to induce the reader to continue reading beyond the headline. (In the case of a negative type of "warning" headline we might even draw a further analogy and go so far as to say that it is then more in the nature of a *red* flag.)

It is obvious, therefore, that there are two principal attributes of good headlines. They select, from the total readership of the publication, those readers who are (or can be induced to be) interested in the subject of the advertisement. And they promise them a worthwhile reward for reading it.

What Kinds of Rewards Do Good Headlines Promise?

In this chapter we are going to concentrate upon one hundred examples of the two types of headlines which *in toto* unquestionably have the best record of resultfulness, based upon criteria which will soon be described.

Both types promise desirable rewards for reading. One does it through a positive approach, the other through a negative one. Here is how they do it:

> 1. By managing to convey, in a few words, how the reader can save, gain, or accomplish something through the use of your product—how it will *increase* this: his mental, physical, financial, social, emotional, or spiritual stimulation, satisfaction, well-being, or security.
>
> 2. Or, negatively, by pointing out how the reader can avoid (reduce or eliminate) risks, worries, losses, mistakes, embarrassment, drudgery, or some other undesirable condition through the use of your product—how it will *decrease* this: his fear of poverty, illness, or accident, discomfort, boredom, and the loss of business or social prestige or advancement.

As you review these one hundred headlines you will notice how many of them manage to go even one desirable step further. They also tell how quickly, easily, or inexpensively the promise will be performed. And, as you will see, they are not claim-and-boast headlines, which research by Gallup-Robinson indicates are "roughly only 60% as effective as consumer-benefit headlines."

WHY THESE HEADLINES WERE SELECTED

The one hundred headlines which follow were selected for review in this chapter because, first, each provides *in itself* a little lesson in headline writing; second, because most of them are backed up by a record of resultfulness sufficiently noteworthy to merit their analysis and study. This record is either based upon the high readership rating of the ad they headlined or (in the case of ads which carried a key number) based upon the profitable number of inquiries or orders they produced for the advertiser. The inclusion of the very few not in either of these two categories was based upon many years of day-by-day working experience devoted to headlines.

Some of them are new, recently used; others are not. But all are as immutably timeless and changeless as human nature itself in exemplifying how to make a headline capture attention and arouse interest.

One of them is what is generally called a "curiosity" headline. That type of headline is commonly used and thus should be represented here. Yet, merely to excite curiosity, such headlines all too often introduce ideas entirely unrelated to the product, its functions, and the advantages of owning it.

By so doing, they arouse an irrelevant and spurious kind of curiosity—one which cannot, with the greatest possible effectiveness, be followed through with the body copy that must try to turn idle curiosity into desire-to-purchase action.

Also (and of major importance) you may perhaps read a "curiosity-headlined" ad if you *have* time. But, for an ad whose headline promises you some benefit you truly want, you are much more likely to try to *make* time!

The success of all of these headlines was due mainly to the headline itself—rather than to an extraordinary quality of copy. That is why such notable ads as *The Penalty of Leadership, The Priceless Ingredient, Somewhere West of Laramie* (and others characterized by superlative body copy) have not been included.

Likewise, their effectiveness was not due in inordinate measure to any supporting picture or art work—nor to any trick gimmicks of layout which almost make it stand on its head in an attempt to force attention. In other words, the headline was good enough, alone, to get attention and to induce the reader to keep reading.

100 Good Headlines and Why They Were so Profitable

Now that we've written a good reference for these particular headlines, let us review them and try to discover why they were so effective.

Occasionally, as we go along, we'll take a breather. First, as a time-out period. Second, so that we can make what might be called some General Observations about Specific Elements, about certain of the elements present in so many of the headlines. In that way we can point them up, because they are worth stressing, and we can also avoid having continually to draw your attention to them.

The headlines advertise many different kinds of products. Some are sold in retail stores, some by sales representatives, some by mail direct to the customer. But regardless of what the product is, or how it is sold, the principles discussed here apply.

Now put on your spiked shoes. We're going to "run the hundred." That will enable us to learn by actual example, instead of through a long and less interesting discussion of general precepts.

1.   THE SECRET OF MAKING PEOPLE LIKE YOU

Almost $500,000 was spent profitably to run keyed ads displaying this headline. It drew many hundreds of thousands of readers into the body matter of a "people-mover" advertisement—one which, by itself, built a big business. Pretty irresistible headline, isn't it?

2.   A LITTLE MISTAKE THAT COST A FARMER $3,000 A YEAR

A sizable appropriation was spent successfully in farm magazines on this ad. Sometimes the negative idea of offsetting, reducing, or eliminating the "risk of loss" is even more attractive to the reader than the "prospect of gain."

As the great business executive Chauncey Depew once said, "I would not stay up all of one night to make $100; but I would stay up all of seven nights to keep from losing it." As Walter Horvath says in *Six Successful Selling Techniques,* "People will fight much harder to avoid losing something they *already own* than to gain something of greater value that they do *not* own." It is also true that they have the feeling that losses and waste can often be more easily retrieved than new profits can be gained.

What farmer could pass up reading the copy under such a headline —to find out: "What was the mistake? Why was it 'little'? Am *I* making it? If it cost that farmer a loss of $3,000 a year maybe it's costing me a lot more! Perhaps the copy will also tell me about other mistakes *I* might be making."

3.　　ADVICE TO WIVES WHOSE HUSBANDS DON'T SAVE MONEY—BY
　　　　A WIFE

The headline strength of the word "advice" has often been proven. Most people want it, regardless of whether or not they follow it. And the particular "ailment" referred to is common enough to interest a lot of readers. The "it happened to me" tag line, "by a Wife," increases the desire to read the copy. (This ad far outpulled the advertiser's previous best ad, *Get Rid of Money Worries.*)

4.　　THE CHILD WHO WON THE HEARTS OF ALL

This was a keyed-result ad which proved spectacularly profitable. It appeared in women's magazines. The emotional-type copy described (and the photograph portrayed) the kind of little girl any parent would want his daughter to be. Laughing, rollicking, running forward, with arms outstretched, right out of the ad and into the arms and heart of the reader.

5.   ARE YOU EVER TONGUE-TIED AT A PARTY?

Pinpoints the myriads of self-conscious, inferiority-complexed wallflowers. "That's me! I want to read this ad; maybe it tells me exactly what to do about it."

As you go along you will notice how many of these headlines are interrogative ones. They ask a question to which people want to read the answer. They excite curiosity and interest in the body matter which follows. They hit home—cut through verbose indirectness. The best ones are challenges which are difficult to ignore, cannot be dismissed with a quick no or yes and without further reading, are pertinent and relevant to the reader. Note how many of the ones included here measure up to these specifications.

6.   HOW A NEW DISCOVERY MADE A PLAIN GIRL BEAUTIFUL

Wide appeal: there are more plain girls than beautiful ones—and just about all of them want to be better looking.

7.   HOW TO WIN FRIENDS AND INFLUENCE PEOPLE

This helped to sell millions of copies of the book of the same title. Strong basic appeal: we all want to do it. But without the words "how to" the headline would become simply a trite wall motto.

8.   THE LAST 2 HOURS ARE THE LONGEST—AND THOSE ARE THE 2 HOURS YOU SAVE

An airline ad featured a faster jet-powered flight. Headline is a bull's-eye for air-experienced travelers who know what those last two interminable hours can do to their nerves and patience. Like many fine headlines, it doubtless came right out of the personal experience of its writer.

This headline (and all the others discussed here) would have been good even if it had not been supported by any picture at all. But its effect was heightened by a photo of a wrist watch with the hour marks indicating 1 to 10 bunched together—and 10, 11, and 12 stretched wide apart.

9.   WHO ELSE WANTS A SCREEN STAR FIGURE?

Who doesn't? Except men—and this successful and much-run ad is not addressed to them. "Who else" also has a "get on the bandwagon" connotation: not "*can* it be done?" but "*who else* wants to have it?"

10.   DO YOU MAKE THESE MISTAKES IN ENGLISH?

A direct challenge. Now read the headline back, eliminating that vital word "these." This word is the "hook" that almost forces you into the copy. "What are these particular mistakes? Do I make them?" Also notice (as with many of the other headlines reviewed) that this one promises to provide helpful personal information *in its own context,* not merely "advertising talk."

The Attraction of the Specific

In this first breather let us stop to impress upon your mind how significant a part the "specific" plays in so many good headlines. It appears in many of our first ten. And it will appear in a surprising number of the next ninety. You will see how magnetically it helps to draw the reader into the body matter of an advertisement.

So notice, as you continue reading, how many of these headlines contain specific words or phrases that make the ad promise to tell you: How, Here's, These, Which, Which of These, Who, Who Else, Where, When, What, Why. Also note how frequently exact amounts are used: number of days, evenings, hours, minutes, dollars, ways, types of. This "attraction of the specific" is worth your special attention—not only as relating to words and phrases but also concerning headline ideas themselves. For example, compare the appeal of

"We'll Help You Make More Money" with "We'll Help You Pay the Rent."

11. WHY SOME FOODS "EXPLODE" IN YOUR STOMACH

A provocative "why" headline. Based upon the completely understandable fact that some food combinations virtually "explode" in the stomach. Broad appeal. (Relevant picture of chemical retort shaped like a stomach, starting to explode.)

12. HANDS THAT LOOK LOVELIER IN 24 HOURS—OR YOUR MONEY BACK

Universal appeal to women. Result guaranteed: "Or Your Money Back."

13. YOU CAN LAUGH AT MONEY WORRIES—IF YOU FOLLOW THIS SIMPLE PLAN

Something everybody wants to be able to do. A successful keyed ad upon which many thousands have been spent.

14. WHY SOME PEOPLE ALMOST ALWAYS MAKE MONEY IN THE STOCK MARKET

A profitable checked-result ad selling a book written by a partner in a well-known and highly regarded brokerage house. Important key words: "some" and "almost"—which make the headline credible.

15. WHEN DOCTORS "FEEL ROTTEN" THIS IS WHAT THEY DO

What's the secret of the success of this well-known ad? First: the suggestion of paradox. We seldom think of doctors as being in poor health themselves. And when they are, what they do about it is information "right from the horse's mouth"; carries a note of authority and greater assurance of "reward for reading the ad." Note the positive promise of reward in "This Is What They Do."

Also, the use of the unabashed colloquialism "feel rotten" gets attention; sounds human, natural. Besides, it has surprise value—since the vocabulary of the advertising pages has a certain sameness and stilted quality. Many a headline fails to stop readers because its vocabulary is so hackneyed. No word or phrase in it has any attention-arresting element of surprise, no words, expressions, or ideas not commonly used or expected in the headline of an advertisement.

This ad pulled only half the number of responses when a test was made changing "When Doctors Feel Rotten" to "When Doctors Don't Feel Up to Par." (Other examples of the use of common colloquialisms and surprise words are given, and commented upon, in many of these good headlines.)

Since this idea of using headline words not commonly utilized in the lexicon of advertising is worth such serious consideration, let us cite a few more examples. For a book on scientific weight control: the one word "Pot-Belly"! (Not very elegant, but it proved an effective stopper.) For a dictionary: a single word (onion, hog, shad, pelican, skunk, kangaroo, etc.) as the bold-face headline of each in a series of small-space advertisements. You couldn't miss it on the page and you wanted to know what it was all about. The copy followed through by illustrating how simple and clear were the definitions in that particular dictionary. For a book of golf instruction: "Don't Belly-Ache About Your Golf *This* Year!"

16.   IT SEEMS INCREDIBLE THAT YOU CAN OFFER THESE
          SIGNED ORIGINAL ETCHINGS—FOR ONLY $5 EACH!

Anticipates the reader's natural incredulity concerning such an exceptional bargain. Thus helps to overcome his doubt in advance, by acknowledging the likelihood of it.

17. FIVE FAMILIAR SKIN TROUBLES—WHICH DO YOU WANT TO OVERCOME?

"Let me keep reading—to see if I have one of the five." The old "which of these" selling technique; not "*do* you want?" but "*which* do you want?" (Interrogative headline helps entice readers into the copy. Note how many of these hundred are interrogative headlines.)

18. WHICH OF THESE $2.50-TO-$5 BEST SELLERS DO YOU WANT —FOR ONLY $1 EACH?

This keyed ad sold hundreds of thousands of books. Strong comparative-price bargain appeal.

19. WHO EVER HEARD OF A WOMAN LOSING WEIGHT—AND ENJOYING 3 DELICIOUS MEALS AT THE SAME TIME?

Another example of a headline which anticipates incredulity in order to help overcome it.

20. HOW I IMPROVED MY MEMORY IN ONE EVENING

This is the famous "Addison Sims of Seattle" ad which coined that household phrase. Could *you* escape wanting to read it?

21. DISCOVER THE FORTUNE THAT LIES HIDDEN IN YOUR SALARY

One of those good "discover what lies hidden" headlines. (Note others here.) A proven puller for an advertiser offering sound securities on a "pay out of income" basis.

22.   DOCTORS PROVE 2 OUT OF 3 WOMEN CAN HAVE MORE BEAU-
TIFUL SKIN IN 14 DAYS

Women want it. "Why two out of three? Am *I* one of the two? How have doctors proved it? Quick results are what I want . . . Only fourteen days!"

How Many Words Should a Headline Contain?

You have probably often read about the desirability of having no more than a certain number of words in your headline. Yet, in this second breather, we want to point out that many of the headlines already quoted (and others to follow) are, by ordinary standards, quite long. Yet, despite their length, they were successful.

Obviously, it is not wise to make a headline any lengthier than its primary function actually requires. However, greater-than-usual length need not worry you . . . provided the headline's high spots of interest are physically well broken up and clearly displayed—and provided the personal advantages promised to the reader are presented so appositely that it is almost as though his own name appeared in the headline.

Worth recounting is the story of Max Hart (of Hart, Schaffner & Marx) and his advertising manager, the late and great George L. Dyer. They were arguing about long copy. To clinch the argument Mr. Dyer said, "I'll bet you $10 I can write a newspaper page of solid type and you'd read every word of it."

Mr. Hart scoffed at the idea. "I don't have to write a line of it to prove my point," Mr. Dyer responded. "I'll only tell you the headline. That would be "This page is all about Max Hart!"

23.   HOW I MADE A FORTUNE WITH A "FOOL IDEA"

Paradoxes excite interest. Broad appeal: almost everyone has once had a pet money-making idea that others have thought foolish and impractical. Sympathy for the underdog: "What's the story of this man who 'turned the tables' on the people who ridiculed him?"

24. HOW OFTEN DO YOU HEAR YOURSELF SAYING: "NO, I HAVEN'T READ IT; I'VE BEEN MEANING TO!"

A well-known book club has spent a great deal of money on this ad. Headline aimed accurately at its large market—people who "mean to" keep up with the new books but somehow "never get around to it."

25. THOUSANDS HAVE THIS PRICELESS GIFT—BUT NEVER DISCOVER IT!

"What 'priceless gift'? Why is it 'priceless'? If 'thousands' have it perhaps I have it too."
The "undiscovered" angle has great attraction. Legions of people are convinced that they possess talents and abilities which others have never discovered. Consequently, their world is unfortunately inclined to underrate or misjudge them.

26. WHOSE FAULT WHEN CHILDREN DISOBEY?

What parent wouldn't be stopped cold by this headline? *"I'm* the one who's probably to blame. It's a distressing condition—and, most important, a reflection upon *me.* Maybe this ad tells me what to do about it."

27. HOW A "FOOL STUNT" MADE ME A STAR SALESMAN

"What is the 'fool stunt'? Why did people call it that? How did it transform this fellow? I'd like to be able to 'sell' myself and my ideas—even though selling may not be my vocation." (A large expenditure was made profitably on this ad after its resultfulness had been proven.)

28.   HAVE YOU THESE SYMPTOMS OF NERVE EXHAUSTION?

Everyone likes to read about his "symptoms." The appeal is broad; the condition of "nerve exhaustion" is common.

29.   GUARANTEED TO GO THRU ICE, MUD, OR SNOW—OR WE PAY THE TOW!

If you offer a powerful guarantee with your product, play it up strongly and quickly in the headline. Don't relegate it to minor display. Many products are actually backed up by dramatic guarantees —but their advertising does not make the most of them.

30.   HAVE YOU A "WORRY" STOCK?

"Perhaps this ad will tell me why I need not lose any sleep over it —or how I can replace it with one that will zoom."

31.   HOW A NEW KIND OF CLAY IMPROVED MY COMPLEXION IN 30 MINUTES

Promises a desirable reward for reading. And the true experience of another person (*with something relevant to our own desires*) is always interesting.

32.   161 NEW WAYS TO A MAN'S HEART—IN THIS FASCINATING BOOK FOR COOKS

Again the attraction of the specific—tied up with a strong basic appeal.

33.   PROFITS THAT LIE HIDDEN IN YOUR FARM

Widely run in farm papers, with exceptional results. The hidden-profit idea and the suggestion of retrieving a loss.

34.   IS THE LIFE OF A CHILD WORTH $1 TO YOU?

Trenchant headline for a brake-relining service. Strong emotional appeal: how the life of a little child may be snuffed out by an accident due to *your* ineffective brakes.

35.   EVERYWHERE WOMEN ARE RAVING ABOUT THIS AMAZING NEW SHAMPOO!

The colloquial: "raving about." The "success" word: "everywhere." (The increasing popularity and sale of a product are adduced as evidence of its merit. "Nothing succeeds like success"; and people love to climb on a bandwagon.) And the overworked "amazing" still seems to have some power left.

36.   DO YOU DO ANY OF THESE TEN EMBARRASSING THINGS?

Bull's-eye question. All of us are afraid of embarrassing ourselves before others; being criticized, looked down upon, talked about. "Which 'ten' are they? Do *I* do any of them?"

37.   SIX TYPES OF INVESTORS—WHICH GROUP ARE YOU IN?

This ad produced inquiries in large quantities. Investors reviewed the characteristics of each of the six groups, as described in the ad, then inquired about a program designed to meet the investment purposes of their particular group.

The Primary Viewpoint—The "Point of You"

Breather No. 3 is a short one because you already know its "lesson" very well. But to stress its importance let us point out this to you: *43 of these 100 headlines contain one of these actual words—"you," "your," or "yourself";* Even when the pronoun is first person singular (for example, *How I Improved My Memory in One Evening*), the reward promised is so universally desired that it is, in effect, really saying, "You can do it too!"

Thousands of words have already been written about the "point of you"—but let me remind you that, given a fountain pen, 96 per cent of 500 college women wrote their own names; shown a map of the U.S.A., 447 men out of 500 looked first for the location of their home towns! Harold Barnes, of the American Newspaper Publishers' Association, really was on target when he said: "To call up an image of the reader, all you need to do is pin up a target. Then, starting at the outside, you can label his interests in this order: the world, the United States, his home state, his home town, and we'll lump together in the black center his family and himself. . . . me. Myself. I come first. I am the bull's-eye."

38.   HOW TO TAKE OUT STAINS . . . USE (PRODUCT NAME)
         AND FOLLOW THESE EASY DIRECTIONS

An example of a good "service" ad—one which, besides being relevantly tied up with the product, also contains helpful information usable in itself. (Such ads often have considerable longevity because they are cut out and used for future reference.)

39.   TODAY . . . ADD $10,000 TO YOUR ESTATE—
         FOR THE PRICE OF A NEW HAT

Who wouldn't want to do that? Doubt as to the promise is offset by the fact that the advertiser is a large and reputable insurance company.

40.   DOES YOUR CHILD EVER EMBARRASS YOU?

Direct, challenging, a common circumstance. Brings up a flood of recollections. How can such unpleasant experiences be avoided in the future?

Based upon a strong selfish appeal. Parents are, first, individuals; second, parents. The kind of reflection that children cast upon the prestige and self-esteem of their parents is a useful copy angle to remember. (This headline is the negative opposite of No. 4, *The Child Who Won the Hearts of All.*)

41. IS YOUR HOME PICTURE-POOR?

A rifle-shot question hitting thousand's of readers. Illustrated by photo of an otherwise attractive living room with blank areas on its walls; with X's indicating where pictures would improve the room's appearance.

42. HOW TO GIVE YOUR CHILDREN EXTRA IRON—
    THESE 3 DELICIOUS WAYS

It obeys the wise maximum of newspaper reporters: "Start where the reader is." In other words, the public already accepts the fact that children's blood should contain plenty of iron. So the headline goes on from there—promising "extra" iron and "3 delicious ways" to get it (*"delicious"* ways; so not the common parent vs. child battle).

43. TO PEOPLE WHO WANT TO WRITE—BUT CAN'T GET STARTED

Unerringly selects its audience, which is large—and stymied.

44. THIS ALMOST-MAGICAL LAMP LIGHTS HIGHWAY TURNS
    BEFORE YOU MAKE THEM

The word "almost" lends believability. Headline promises an automatic no-effort method of relieving an annoying condition or avoiding a dangerous emergency.

45.　THE CRIMES WE COMMIT AGAINST OUR STOMACHS

Another "start where the reader is" headline—because most people already believe they often give their digestive processes some pretty rough treatment. This rapport, between the theme of the ad and the common belief of its readers, makes the "we" and "our" practically equal in effectiveness to "you" and "your."

46.　THE MAN WITH THE "GRASSHOPPER MIND"

An immediate association with himself leaps to the mind of the reader. He wants to check at once on the personal parallel. What are the symptoms? Starting things one never finishes? Jumping from one thing to another?

"How much am I like him? It's not a good trait. What did he do about it?" This is an example of a negative headline that strikes home more accurately and dramatically than would a positive one.

47.　THEY LAUGHED WHEN I SAT DOWN AT THE PIANO— BUT WHEN I STARTED TO PLAY!

Another one that has entered our language. Sympathy with the underdog. Particularly interesting, structurally, as an example of a headline which "turns the corner" by using a final tag line to make itself positive instead of negative.

Also worth remembering: the before-and-after angle can be effective in many headlines.

48.　THROW AWAY YOUR OARS!

Short and positive commands often make good *stopper* headlines. When Ole Evinrude, the outboard-motor king, ran a small ad with this headline he took the first step toward building his one-room machine shop into a big business. (A similar headline, *Throw Away*

Your Aerial!, was also once responsible for building a business in the radio field.)

This type of headline is worth thinking about when the product you are advertising eliminates the need for some heretofore necessary piece of equipment, some onerous job, or some sizable item of expense.

49. HOW TO DO WONDERS WITH A LITTLE LAND!

A successful headline which pulled 75 per cent better than *Two Acres and Security* and 40 per cent better than *A Little Land—a Lot of Living*. The reason: "how to" and "do wonders with."

50. WHO ELSE WANTS LIGHTER CAKE—IN HALF THE MIXING TIME?

Strong appeal. Another good "who else" headline. (*No. 9, Who Else Wants a Screen Star Figure?*)

51. LITTLE LEAKS THAT KEEP MEN POOR

A keyed "retrieving a loss" ad whose checked resultfulness justified frequent repetition.

52. PIERCED BY 301 NAILS . . . RETAINS FULL AIR PRESSURE

Who wouldn't be interested in reading more about a tire like this?

53. NO MORE BACK-BREAKING GARDEN CHORES FOR ME—YET OURS IS NOW THE SHOW-PLACE OF THE NEIGHBORHOOD!

A good example of a before-and-after headline which makes the turn from negative to positive. Also worth noting: it has an effective element of excitement in it—a feature of many good headlines, communicating the copywriter's enthusiasm to the printed page.

Don't Worry about a "Negative" Approach

This breather No. 4 is about negative headlines. "Accentuate the positive; eliminate the negative," said a popular song of some years ago. For years that has also been the popular refrain of the advice often given to copywriters. Discussion about negative headlines has sometimes sparked more fire than enlightenment.

Yet our 100 headlines include 21 which are completely negative and 10 others which start with a negative approach and then become positive. So the negative approach must have *some* good reason for existence. It has. What is it?

One of the principal objectives of a headline is to strike as directly as possible right at a situation confronting the reader. Sometimes you can do this with greater accuracy if you use a negative headline which pinpoints his ailment rather than the alleviation of it. (For example, *Is YOUR home Picture-Poor?—Have YOU a "Worry" Stock?— Little Leaks That Keep Men Poor.*)

So when you face that kind of situation don't be afraid to "accentuate the negative."

Now let's proceed to another great headline which captured a place in our everyday language.

54.　　OFTEN A BRIDESMAID, NEVER A BRIDE

So poignantly true, so pointed—and so common.

55.　　HOW MUCH IS "WORKER TENSION" COSTING YOUR COMPANY?

An ad which was successful in business magazines reaching executives. "I want to know which are the kinds of 'worker tension' specifically. What is 'worker tension' costing other companies in net profits? How much is it costing us? If it is, what can we do about it?"

56.   TO MEN WHO WANT TO QUIT WORK SOMEDAY

Selects its readers without wasting a word. (And who can say that the audience isn't kind of large?)

57.   HOW TO PLAN YOUR HOUSE TO SUIT YOURSELF

This pulled almost 20 per cent better than *How to Avoid These Mistakes in Planning Your Home.* Apparently, people expect the architect to avoid the mistakes—but feel that they themselves know better than anyone else what will best suit their particular needs and preferences.

58.   BUY NO DESK . . . UNTIL YOU'VE SEEN THIS SENSATION
    OF THE BUSINESS SHOW

Strong "stopper" type of "command" headline, adaptable for many uses. Copy quickly follows with "until you have checked as to whether it has this feature, and this one, and this . . ."

59.   CALL BACK THESE GREAT MOMENTS AT THE OPERA

Sometimes it's a good idea to "start where the reader *was.*" This nostalgic headline was used to sell phonograph records of great operas. The idea can be used in a positive way: tying up with a desirable remembrance. Or it can be used negatively: contrasting a certain new product advantage with an undesirable remembrance.

60.   "I LOST MY BULGES . . . AND SAVED MONEY TOO"

Word "bulges" is a stopper, not commonly used in advertising's lexicon. Double-edged appeal: the promise to end an unwanted condition and to save you money also.

61. WHY (BRAND NAME) BULBS GIVE MORE LIGHT THIS YEAR

This one illustrates an important point, one which many advertisers hate to swallow. It is usually not a good idea to tell the name of the company (or the brand name) in the headline—or to make it tell too much of the story. When this is done right in the headline itself it often gives the whole thing away and does not tempt the reader into the copy.

However, as in this case, when the advertiser is a nationally famous company (particularly when it is noted for its enterprise, innovations, improvements, and research), the use of the company, or brand name can add *news* value to the headline—and help to substantiate the truth of the claim made in it.

62. RIGHT AND WRONG FARMING METHODS—AND LITTLE
POINTERS THAT WILL INCREASE YOUR PROFITS

Exceedingly profitable in farm papers. A combination of negative and positive appeals, with a lot of "come hither" for farmers.

63. NEW CAKE-IMPROVER GETS YOU COMPLIMENTS GALORE!

There are three things which advertising can tell its readers: (1) what the product *is;* (2) what it *does;* and . . . this headline utilizes the third (and often overlooked) one:

In terms of the advertiser it is this: What *other* people will say of you, think of you, do for you—how they will admire you, envy you, imitate you—because of what *my* product can accomplish for you. In terms of the prospective customer it is this: Because of what your product can do *for* me, people may think more *of* me!

This third factor (which is an extension of the No. 2 factor mentioned above) can be made so effective, and is so often neglected that it rates special attention here as Breather No. 5. The proper use of it can make advertising copy make more sales. Therefore, it is worth a prominent niche in your memory.

To keep it there, visualize a somewhat ridiculous picture. (Tying up an absurd pictorial association with a concept you want to remember is of course a well-known aid to memory.) The sketch is of a boy sitting on the prow of a PT boat. His mother is sitting in the stern. Between the two the initials "PT" are printed in big letters on the side of this type of small but very fast patrol boat used so extensively in World War II in the South Pacific. This mental picture will help you remember the initials "BOY PT MOM." And these are the initials of the phrase "Because Of You, People Think More Of Me."

Headline No. 63 utilizes that factor. It promises the reader that this new cake improver will win her compliments from others; that because of *you* (the advertiser) other people will think more of *her* (the reader). You are offering to show her how to make what she might later call her "reputation cake."

Sometimes this element in copy is called the "prestige factor," and is considered only as an extension of the "what the product does" type of copy. (In discussing the advertising of ladies' perfumes Hal Stebbins calls it "selling the effect of the effect.") In the advertising of a great many products, it can be made so persuasive, so compelling, that it rates at least a subcategory of its own.

64.   IMAGINE ME . . . HOLDING AN AUDIENCE SPELLBOUND FOR 30 MINUTES!

A profitable narrative-ad headline. Broad interest in this kind of ability. Narrator's surprise and apparent humility lend credence and humanness to the statement.

65.   THIS IS MARIE ANTOINETTE—RIDING TO HER DEATH

An often-repeated ad for a set of books. It pulled eight times as many responses in ¼-page size as were ever received from a double-spread.

This is the only straight "curiosity" headline included here. Its headline was relevant—not, as so commonly used, one of those trick devices to force attention when advertising a product not closely related to the headline.

66. DID YOU EVER SEE A "TELEGRAM" FROM YOUR HEART?

A real stopper of a headline, with a great deal of lure in the copy. Top picture shows a cardiogram report printed upon a Western Union telegram form.

67. NOW ANY AUTO REPAIR JOB CAN BE "DUCK SOUP" FOR YOU

What do you know—the words "duck soup" in an ad! But doesn't it tell the story in a more unusual way than would "easy," "simple," or some such word—particularly to the type of market at which this ad is aimed?

68. NEW SHAMPOO LEAVES YOUR HAIR SMOOTHER—
EASIER TO MANAGE

A result that all women want is clearly and persuasively stated. Word "leaves" makes it sound effortless.

69. IT'S A SHAME FOR YOU NOT TO MAKE GOOD MONEY—
WHEN THESE MEN DO IT SO EASILY

The colloquial "it's a shame." Sympathetic understanding of the reader: "You are as capable as these other men." (Headline, of course, is supported by photos and good testimonials.)

70. YOU NEVER SAW SUCH LETTERS AS HARRY AND I
GOT ABOUT OUR PEARS

Friendly, human, disarmingly ingenuous, refreshingly non-"advertisy" in language. And, of course, the reference to "such letters."

71.   THOUSANDS NOW PLAY WHO NEVER
        THOUGHT THEY COULD

A headline perennially profitable for a large music school. Again, the copy is crammed with testimonials and references substantiating the claim.

72.   GREAT NEW DISCOVERY KILLS KITCHEN ODORS QUICK!—
        MAKES INDOOR AIR "COUNTRY-FRESH"

The headline of an ad that launched a big business. Faces a common problem head-on; offers an easy and pleasant solution.

73.   MAKE THIS 1-MINUTE TEST—OF AN AMAZING
        NEW KIND OF SHAVING CREAM

The "make this test" angle has been used in many good headlines. It is widely usable for others. Its purpose is to induce the reader to participate in a demonstration of the product's merits. However, if credible and dramatic, the test can represent a persuasive demonstration whether or not the reader ever actually makes it.

74.   ANNOUNCING . . . THE NEW EDITION OF THE
        ENCYCLOPEDIA THAT MAKES IT FUN TO LEARN THINGS

The "announcement" type of headline (when bringing out a new product) wins attention because people are interested in new things.

Neophobia?—Americans Don't Suffer from
This *Ailment!*

Breather No. 6 is here to remind you that in a great many of these headlines you find the word new—or connotation of it, such as "new kind of," "new discovery," "new way to," etc. Americans are partial to the new or novel; they do not suffer from neophobia. To them the mere factor of newness seems to be prima facie evidence of "betterness."

Undeviating affection for the old and tried may be strong in other countries; in ours the desire to try the new is stronger. The great achievements of our inventors and enterprising manufacturers have trained us to believe that if it's new it's likely to be better. However, the word "new" in a headline should be backed up by copy pointing out the merits of something *really* new and advantageous, not some transparently trivial difference.

And now we come to another familiar headline . . .

75.   AGAIN SHE ORDERS . . . "A CHICKEN SALAD, PLEASE"

You still hear it quoted. It sold hundreds of thousands of copies of an etiquette book because it capsulized a common and embarrassing situation.

76.   FOR THE WOMAN WHO IS OLDER THAN SHE LOOKS

This headline was a stopper to thousands . . . and more successful than the subtly different *For the Woman Who Looks Younger than She Is.*

77.   WHERE YOU CAN GO IN A GOOD USED CAR

The headline of an excellent advertisement which featured what the product *does*—rather than what it *is*. It appeared years ago, before practically everyone owned an automobile. Underneath the headline was a picture of the Indiana Sand Dunes, followed by good copy about the dunes and pointing out that "A good used car brings the whole country to you and yours. Why not buy one? You don't need a lot of money." Finally, after selling the *idea,* the copy gave some specific details about the cars which were for sale.

78.   CHECK THE KIND OF BODY YOU WANT

Check list displayed at top immediately invites reader's participation in specifying "which of these" improvements he would like to make in his physique. Keyed ad repeated frequently by well-known physical culturist.

79.   "YOU KILL THAT STORY—OR I'LL RUN YOU OUT OF THE STATE!"

A true-narrative ad run by a nation-wide chain of newspapers. Could you flip over the page without wanting to know what happened?

80.   HERE'S A QUICK WAY TO BREAK UP A COLD

In simple everyday words, a direct promise to end an undesirable condition—quickly.

81.   THERE'S ANOTHER WOMAN WAITING FOR EVERY MAN—
         AND SHE'S TOO SMART TO HAVE "MORNING MOUTH"

Had quite an impact on women readers, this toothpaste ad. Obviously, for there surely is a lot of motivation in its theme: "No woman wants her husband to carry the memory of her morning breath to work with him. The attractive women he meets during the day don't have it."

Stale News to the Advertiser May Be Fresh News to the Reader

And now we come to Breather No. 7. Don't think that because it is our last one it is of least importance. In fact, its value becomes apparent when you realize how many of these headlines employ it. "Get *news* (or news value) into your headline" is probably the best way to define it.

Since you can't pack everything into a headline, stick to your principal appeal—but give it news value if you can. And remember that what may be stale news to the advertiser may be fresh news to the reader. The advertiser is of course thoroughly familiar with his manufacturing methods, the ingredients he uses, the functions of his product. They may have no news value for him. They may even be similar to those of his competitors. But that is not true of the readers of his advertisements. Something about the product or the service it renders may be entirely new and sensationally persuasive to the public. And the advertiser who features it first captures its appeal for himself, regardless of the "me too" efforts of competitors who may have heretofore failed to capitalize upon it.

82.   THIS PEN "BURPS" BEFORE IT DRINKS—
          BUT NEVER AFTERWARDS!

Headline expressed in a few words a copy theme credited with pushing one brand of fountain pen up to a leading position.

83.   IF YOU WERE GIVEN $200,000 TO SPEND—ISN'T THIS THE
          KIND OF (TYPE OF PRODUCT, BUT NOT BRAND NAME)
          YOU WOULD BUILD?

A "self-incriminating" (and widely applicable) way to have the reader help to specify what he himself would value most in such a product.

The copy follows through along these lines: Surely you would put *this* feature into it. You would be sure that it brought you *this* advantage, and this, and this. . . . Well, we've done it all *for* you. As you can see, this product was really created for *you!*

84.   "LAST FRIDAY . . . WAS I SCARED!—MY BOSS ALMOST
          FIRED ME!"

A human narrative people wanted to read because it did—or could —"happen to me."

85.   67 REASONS WHY IT WOULD HAVE PAID YOU TO ANSWER
       OUR AD A FEW MONTHS AGO

An interesting example of an ad that backtracks—pointing out in detail what the reader has missed by not buying the product before. A frequently repeated ad used by a well-known news magazine to pull for subscriptions.

86.   SUPPOSE THIS HAPPENED ON **YOUR** WEDDING DAY!

A profitable narrative-ad headline which makes it pretty hard to flip the page. "What was this tragic happening? Could it—or did it—happen to me?"

87.   DON'T LET ATHLETE'S FOOT "LAY YOU UP"

This pulled three times better than *Relieve Foot Itch*. It gives the disease a relevant name, points out its unwanted effect.

88.   ARE THEY BEING PROMOTED RIGHT OVER YOUR HEAD?

Another question aimed at a big target: the legion of frustrated, discouraged people who feel that their ability and conscientiousness are not being amply rewarded by recognition and advancement. (Frequently run by an educational institution which checks the resultfulness of its advertisements.)

89.   ARE WE A NATION OF LOW-BROWS?

This headline helped to sell inexpensive editions of the classics, by the hundreds of thousands. It starts where the reader is—because we, as a nation, are not reputed to be greatly addicted to the high-brow type of literature.

Yet this successful campaign showed that Americans know very well the difference between the meritorious and meretricious—and, if challenged, can prove it with *orders*. The "we" angle avoids the accusatory "you."

90.   A WONDERFUL TWO YEARS' TRIP AT FULL PAY—
         BUT ONLY MEN WITH IMAGINATION CAN TAKE IT

This ad about a course for businessmen was repeated again and again, for a period of seven years, in a long list of magazines. It offers a worth-while reward for reading—with an intriguing challenge in its second line.

91.   WHAT EVERYBODY OUGHT TO KNOW . . . ABOUT THIS STOCK
            AND BOND BUSINESS

The headline of a full-page newspaper ad crammed solid with small-size type—and nary a single picture! It drew 5,000 replies when first published, has since appeared in more than 150 newspapers. Promised helpful information of interest to a large audience. The ad was run by a big investment house.

92.   MONEY-SAVING BARGAINS FROM AMERICA'S OLDEST
            DIAMOND DISCOUNT HOUSE

Of course the "bargain appeal" is sure-fire—and this headline is a good example of straightforward presentation.

93.   FORMER BARBER EARNS $8,000 IN 4 MONTHS
            AS A REAL ESTATE SPECIALIST

Featuring an actual testimonial can make a good headline. In this case, the reader's first reaction is "if a barber can do it maybe I can too!"

94. FREE BOOK—TELLS YOU 12 SECRETS OF
    BETTER LAWN CARE

If you are offering something entirely free (such as a booklet or sample)—and want requests for it in quantity—feature it right in your headline.

95. GREATEST GOLD-MINE OF EASY "THINGS-TO-MAKE"
    EVER CRAMMED INTO ONE BIG BOOK

Perhaps you have a new product (or even an old one) and still lack sufficient accurate data as to which, specifically, are the strongest single selling appeals to feature in your advertising.

In that case, it is often good strategy to "merchandise" the multipurpose "coverage" of your product as thoroughly as you can. By doing so, you avoid the risk of laying too much stress upon any specific appeal which may prove weak or ineffectual. And, by exposing many of your product's uses and advantages, you at least enable your reader to know what they are—so that he can judge for himself the ones which appeal most to him.

96. $80,000 IN PRIZES! HELP US FIND THE NAME FOR
    THESE NEW KITCHENS

No review of good headlines could be considered even fairly representative unless it included an example of one featuring a prize contest. Of course, it first boldly displays how much money can be won; secondly, what you have to do to win some of it.

97. NOW! OWN FLORIDA LAND THIS EASY WAY . . .
    $10 DOWN AND $10 A MONTH

This one also represents a commonly used headline offer—easy terms—and conveys it forcefully and persuasively.

98.   TAKE ANY 3 OF THESE KITCHEN APPLIANCES—
         FOR ONLY $8.95 (VALUES UP TO $15.45)

The familiar reduced-price offer which we see in so many different and alluring forms.

99.   SAVE 20¢ ON 2 CANS OF CRANBERRY SAUCE—
         LIMITED OFFER

An example of the ever-popular coupon-redemption offer. "Limited offer" to increase response. (Sometimes an actual expiration date is stated, to spur quicker action.)

100.   ONE PLACE-SETTING FREE FOR EVERY THREE YOU BUY!

So now we've finished running the hundred—except for this last type of headline: the ubiquitous free offer. The rules specify (as exemplified here) that when something must also be *bought,* this requirement must be displayed with sufficient prominence. "Free" is of course a hackneyed and moss-covered word, but there doesn't seem to be any equally strong or less blatant substitute for it.

MAKING YOUR LAYOUT GET ATTENTION

This book is primarily about *writing* a good advertisement. But this particular chapter is devoted to how to Get Attention—and *both* your headline and your layout play a part in how well you do that.

We have already discussed headlines at length. Now let us make a few observations about attention-winning layouts.

Two Ways to Do It

To get attention with your layout you may do either one of two things:

1. Make it so powerful, so unusual, or so dynamically dominating that it captures the eye despite the competition of other advertisements less unique or less positive in their impact.

2. Or you may make your layout so uncommonly simple, sedate, or "nonprofessional" that its very restraint captures attention.

For example, over a hundred years ago, at London's most fashionable ball, gentlemen were strutting in the most ornate of all the frills and finery in their entire wardrobes. Beau Brummel had not as yet made his entrance. And everyone wondered how that incomparable dandy could possibly "steal *this* show."

Suddenly he appeared. Instantly his figure dominated the whole ballroom. Yet he had merely gone back to simplicity. He was clad in a plainly designed costume of black and white.

Of course, either the first or the second type of layout is an extreme; but the more "neutral" your layout, the more likely it is to be passed by.

DON'T GET "ARTY"

Now, in an effort to get attention with your layout don't try to do it through perfect symmetry and balance.

To get and to hold attention a layout should have two qualities. First, it should be interesting to look at. Second, it should not be static, but should convey the feeling of movement and action, for these are interesting. As the late Professor George Burton Hotchkiss said, "One of the strongest incentives to attention is *movement*."

GETTING INTEREST AND ACTION

Therefore (since interest and action in layouts do help to get and hold the reader's attention), why strain for "perfectly balanced layouts"? Placing your units in artistic symmetry creates a very pretty picture . . . it may be fine art, but is it the best way, or even a good way, to get and hold the reader's attention?

Let us see:

Suppose we illustrate perfect balance by this little circle, divided into evenly balanced units: ⊕ Is it interesting? Does it hold your attention? Does it start your imagination working? No. It just sits there, static, an uninterestingly perfect "balanced layout."

Now compare it with this unevenly divided circle. ⊘ Isn't it more interesting? Doesn't its lack of balance hold your attention longer, start your imagination going?

One of the sagest analysts of effective copy writing, the late E. T. Gundlach expressed it better than I can when he said, "The reason for the superior value of the *un*aesthetic lies in the fact that we notice it. Walk into a room where everything is neatly arranged and your eye may fall upon this or that conspicuously placed chair. But if someone had left a chair upturned in that room you would have seen it instantly. Thus in advertising, it is *ir*-regularity, *dis*-harmony that attracts attention."

And now . . . how much *action* is there in "perfect balance"? Well, perhaps this illustration will give the answer most simply:

So, to get attention with your layout don't get arty. Remember, the principal purpose of a layout is not to win admiration for its own aesthetic beauty but to help to get and hold attention—and thus help your copy win the chance to do a selling job. If it can do that it's beautiful enough for any advertiser!

The Use of Pictures

Do pictures in advertising increase attention value?

Yes. Research demonstrates this fact and also seems to warrant such conclusions as these: pictures of people, children, and animals are natural attention winners; a large, simple picture (especially a photograph) gets more reader attention than several small pictures; a picture of a woman, young child, or baby generally gets greater attention from women than from men; a picture of a man will generally get greater attention from men than from women.

H. W. Hepner of Syracuse University tells us that "In a Gallup survey made of 29,000 individual interviews with readers of twenty different Sunday newspapers located in sixteen cities, it was found that, for rotogravure, people want most to see pictures of other people. The rank order of readers' preferences was (1) photographs of children; (2) groups of adults; (3) sport scenes; (4) animals; and (5) natural scenery." And Mark Wiseman points out that "People are more interested in words combined with pictures than in words alone; more in active-situation pictures than in static, posed ones where nothing interesting is happening."

Show Product in Use

It has also been demonstrated that, when picturing the product in your advertisement, you will get more attention by showing it in use: doing something, accomplishing something for the reader. That, as W. S. Townsend said, "makes it live and breathe and serve right in front of the eyes of the prospect."

It's more appealing to show a bedspread on a bed rather than folded up like a wad of cloth. There's much more "sell" in a hat, suit, or shirt being worn, making a man look keen, neat, successful; in a silver service actually gracing a smart, glistening table; in a soft, cushiony divan cradling a supremely comfortable human being.

"LOOKS TOO MUCH LIKE AN AD"

As you leaf through page after page of advertisements in any magazine, they seem to have a tendency to neutralize the effectiveness of each other. Why? If you were asked to give your answer in a few words you would probably conclude that almost every one "looked too much like an ad"—a carefully calculated, professional job of copywriting and layout-making.

Then suddenly you sometimes come upon an advertisement which doesn't seem to have that word stamped all over it. It has a nonprofessional appearance of spontaneity. It reads as though the advertiser has a genuinely helpful message for you; that, knowing better than anyone else the merits of his product, he might have sat down and written it himself.

STRENGTH—CONTRAST—SIMPLICITY

If your layout is to be strong, make it dominatingly so. Observe the principle of contrast. Whenever the diminutive Napoleon appeared in public he insisted upon being accompanied by his tallest officers. The contrast in height focused attention upon himself. Therefore, if you are going to try to draw attention to your layout through restraint, let it have the stark simplicity which must have made Lincoln stand out powerfully amidst the highly bedecked ambassadors at a diplomatic-corps reception.

And the next time you see an advertisement which does not look so much like a professionally built, technically designed effort to sell, clip it out for your scrapbook. It's worth some study.

What the Illustrations Should (and Should Not) Do

First, an illustration should be relevant to the product, its use, and your copy story about it.

Secondly, an illustration should not be used simply to produce an artistic effect, a decorative touch, or an "atmospheric aura." It should do a specific selling job pictorially, substantiate and advance the copy story. (That is why it is such a wise idea to write the copy first and *then* make the layout.) The selling message is the first consideration, not the technique of presenting it. Your preoccupation should be with the substance, not with the form.

How can illustrations substantiate and advance the copy story? Here are a few suggestions. By showing the product clearly, *preferably in use*. By picturing the advantages of possessing it; or, negatively, the disadvantages of lacking it. By persuasively illustrating the purpose, merit, or function of its design, size, color, ingredients; the craftsmen who make it; the discriminating outlets in which it is sold with noteworthy success.

As Aesop Glim wrote some years ago in one of his "Copy Clinics" in *Printers' Ink*:

Your illustration always has a job to do. It must work for you. It must have an idea to put across. And this idea should point—directly or indirectly—to the desirability of possessing the product or service you are advertising. Rarely, if ever, is your illustration purely an ornament. It is never a work of Art *per se*. Like the copy, the illustration is a means to an end—and never an end in itself.

As a means to an end the illustration may also utilize the principles of showmanship to give even a prosaic product greater glamour and appeal. For example, Henry H. Huff tells us how one salesman did this with an ordinary kitchen utensil:

Two house-to-house salesmen were presenting their wares. One of them unwrapped a wrinkled package, pulled out an aluminum utensil and slammed it down on a table for the housewife's inspection.

The other carefully spread a square of purple velvet upon which he placed, with loving care, a duplicate of the utensil the other salesman was attempting to sell. The salesman who displayed his wares with showmanship rarely lost a sale; the other salesman was a failure.

And now that we've written our headline and finished our layout let us get going on the body-matter copy for our ad—observing Fundamental No. 2: *Show People an Advantage*.

QUIZ ON CHAPTER 1

1. What are five of the fundamentals in the writing of a good advertisement?

2. Which two kinds of rewards do good headlines promise?

3. Why is "the risk of loss" often a more potent appeal than "the prospect of gain"?

4. What is meant by "the attraction of the specific" in headlines?

5. Name some of the words used in many successful headlines.

6. Why is "Primary Viewpoint" so desirable in a headline?

7. Why is a negative approach sometimes more effective?

8. What does "BOY PT MOM" stand for?

9. Which is usually stronger . . . the appeal of that which is new or novel or the affection for the old and tried?

10. Name two good ways to get attention with your layout.

THE "SO WHAT?" DEPARTMENT

Here, for comparison with the hundred headlines reviewed in Chapter 1, are a few of the innumerable *poor* headlines which appeared in expensive advertising space.

In the Freshness of the Morning (A cosmetic advertisement. What will the product do for you? What will it help you to gain?)

Blazing New Trails for 14 Years (Pure "founder's whiskers" —"house talk." The manufacturer is very proud of himself. But where do *you* come in?)

It's the "Little Things" That Count (Count for what?—toward making you healthier, better looking, more successful, more popular? Why not say so?)

What a Difference One Generation Makes (Of course people want different things than they used to. But they want these new things to help them accomplish the same old basic human desires.)

Something They'll All Go For (Why will they? What will this "something" do for you? What's the personal advantage in buying it?)

Beauty Is a Velvet Ribbon (How, why, and how quickly or easily will the product do *what* for your attractiveness?)

Just One Cake of (Brand Name) Soap Can Bring Softer,

Smoother Skin! (That tells the whole story; why read further? Few people will read the text if the headline merely pushes the product. And using the brand name in the headline, expecting it to do a major part of the selling job, is a good way to lose readership at once.)

Their Extra Values Are HIDDEN Values (What are they? Just words? What specific benefits will these extra values bring to you? Even though you may not actually be able to see these hidden values in the physical product itself, you want to know what they are going to mean, in performance, to you personally.)

Beauty and Utility United (Will this "beauty" make your home lovelier, make you prouder to display it to your guests? Will this "utility" save you time, make your work easier? Four frigid words like these won't do much to heat up your desire to read any further copy about the product.)

Anyone Who Knows Can Tell the REAL THING (You don't know. Presumably, the advertising is being run in order to tell you. But what does the headline say? Nothing—except that you apparently are just "not in the know." What advantage does it offer you? None. Will you read any more about it? No.)

You Hear Such Nice Things About It (What things? The gist of at least one of them could surely be headlined in seven appeal-filled words telling "what's in it for *you*.")

America's Thanksgiving Day Starts in the Kitchen (Who could possibly disagree with that flat statement of fact? Flip goes the page.)

Remember when writing your headline: You are really calling out a phrase or a sentence that will "flag" people—and will make as many of them as possible say, "I want that," or at least, "What *is* that? Tell me more."

———

CHAPTER 2

SHOW PEOPLE AN ADVANTAGE

Now we come to the second of our five fundamentals: *Show People an Advantage.* This brings us to the writing of the body-copy matter itself. And Walter Weir certainly got to the heart of it when he said, "Advertising begins and ends with copy—begins with good copy, ends with bad."

Let us say that (as discussed in the first chapter) you *do* get attention—with your headline, your layout, or with both. You've just negotiated the first step. Then, as H. W. Hepner says in his *Effective Advertising,* "catching attention should lead to capturing the mind. Effective advertising means that the reader's mind as well as his eye must be captured." And the psychologist Dr. Donald A. Laird summarized it as follows: "Three out of four readers who notice the advertisement are lost to the average advertiser before they reach the end of it. Capturing attention and holding it are two different things."

"WHAT WILL IT DO FOR ME?"

The thing people want to know above everything else is: What will your product DO for me? To make your copy hold the attention which your layout and headline have already won, show people an advantage—and keep showing them.

For example, do you recall the story of how old Dr. Samuel Johnson auctioned off the contents of the old Anchor Brewery in London?

42

As he stood on the auctioneer's platform, he didn't dwell upon the actual physical fixtures, the complete equipment, the location, the capacity. He didn't orate about what the product intrinsically *was,* but what it would *do* for its purchaser. Here is the sales appeal he boomed out: "We are not here to sell boilers and vats, but the potentiality of growing rich beyond the dreams of avarice." (Actually, about two hundred years ago, it was Dr. Johnson who said, "Promise, large promise, is the soul of an advertisement.")

This principle was so basic that, to emphasize it, I want to cite another example of it which I once read somewhere.

Up New Hampshire way they tell a story of old Daniel Webster, who was asked by a friend to auction his farm. "Neighbors," he said, "we're not auctioning Tom Brown's 34 good milk cows . . . or 80 acres of fine land . . . or a sturdy home that's seen 20 winters. . . .

"No," continued Daniel, "I'm offering you the chance of biting into a red apple with the juicy sap running over your lips . . . the smell of new mown hay . . . clear mountain stream water on your table . . . the crunch of snow under your feet . . . and the best neighbors in the world. . . ."

Daniel's final words hadn't settled on the ground before the bids came in.

You're on Both Sides of the Counter

Of course I know that your copy thoughts are also filled with actual facts about the product itself as merchandise: its wearing qualities, service, tensile strength, ingredients, proofs of value, intrinsic superiority over competitors, etc.

Now (as discussed in the next chapter) these facts are important and you should use them. And here is why and how you will use them: Because, as an advertising man you are, by proxy, both a manufacturer and a consumer. Your role is a double one and you must "dress" for it.

Underneath, you wear your "manufacturer's uniform": a good basic working knowledge of the product and its intrinsic merits as physical merchandise. But, as Christopher Morley once said about people who are trying to sell things, "The customer doesn't give a damn about you until you have aroused his desire." So, *over* your necessary "foundation garment" of factual information, you wear your "consumer's outfit": a clear conception (based on your knowledge of the product itself) of how to portray to consumers, humanly and persuasively, the advantages which the product offers them.

The late Julius Rosenwald put it better than I have (and in a lot fewer words) when, years ago and before Sears went partially retail, he said: "If the firm of Sears, Roebuck had a counter, I would stand on both sides of it."

But many advertisers find it extremely difficult to put themselves on the consumer's side of the counter. Kenneth M. Goode was pointing directly at such advertisers when he wrote: "Nothing of *yours* ever seems half so important to *me* (the consumer) as it does to you. Millions of advertising dollars are wasted every year because what I want to hear has nothing to do with what you want to say."

So when you sit down to a job and think about your headline, your copy, and how you are going to illustrate it, do some of what Kenneth Groesbeck called "television thinking." Visualizing how your story will "go over" with your audience at the receiving end. Remember that you are talking to people in words and pictures—televising to them a paper-and-ink promise to do certain things for them. You are trying to touch them as many times as possible on a point of understanding contact; to make them say, "Yes, that's *me*" or "That's just what *I* do."

What Do People Want?

Now, to make sure that you concentrate upon what the product will do for your reader (or what it will do better than a competing product), let us review the human advantages that people want to gain.

Below is repeated the summarized check list given in Chapter 1. It was given in that chapter because it applies to headlines. It is purposely repeated here because it is so important—and because, of course, it also applies to the writing of your copy. So here is the summary of the two broad generalizations. First, the *plus* one:

Show people—in words, or pictures, or both—what they can save, gain, or accomplish with your product . . . how it will *increase* this: their mental, physical, financial, social, emotional, or spiritual stimulation, satisfaction, self-respect, well-being, or security.

And here is the *minus* generalization:

Show people—in words, or pictures, or both—what risks, worries, losses, mistakes, embarrassments, doubts, drudgery, or other undesirable conditions your product will help them to avoid, lessen, or eliminate . . . how it will *decrease* this: their fear of poverty, illness or accident, discomfort, boredom, offense to others, and the loss of business, personal, or social prestige or advancement.

NOW LET'S GET SPECIFIC

How can you tie up the particular advantages of your product with the personal desires of the greatest number of your readers? This list of strong and specific advertising appeals will help to guide you:

BETTER HEALTH

Greater strength, vigor, endurance. The possibility of longer life.

MORE COMFORT

Ease. Luxury. Self-Indulgences. Convenience.

MORE MONEY

for spending, saving, or giving to others.

MORE LEISURE

for travel, hobbies, rest, play, self-development, etc.

GREATER POPULARITY

through a more attractive personality or through personal accomplishments.

PRIDE OF ACCOMPLISHMENT

Overcoming obstacles and competition. Desire to "do things well."

IMPROVED APPEARANCE

Beauty. Style. Better Physical Build. Cleanliness.

BUSINESS ADVANCEMENT

Better job. Success. "Be your own boss." Reward for merit.

SECURITY IN OLD AGE

Independence. Provision for age or adversity.

SOCIAL ADVANCEMENT

Moving in better circles. Social acceptance. "Keeping up with the Joneses."

PRAISE FROM OTHERS

for one's intelligence, judgment, knowledge, appearance, generosity, or other evidences of superiority.

INCREASED ENJOYMENT

from entertainment, food, drink, and other physical contacts.

And here is a quick check list of some of the other desires most people want to achieve:

Be Good Parents
Have Influence over Others
Be Sociable, Hospitable
Be Gregarious
Express Their Personalities
Resist Domination by Others
Satisfy Their Curiosity
Be Up-to-Date
Emulate What Has General Acceptance as Being Admirable

Appreciate Beauty
Be Proud of Their Possessions
Be Creative
Acquire or Collect Things
Be Efficient
Win Others' Affection
Be "First" in Things
Improve Themselves Mentally
Be Recognized as Authorities

Summing it all up in another convenient form we may (since it is so important) do it in this way:

People Want to GAIN . . . (1) Health (2) Time (3) Money (4) Popularity (5) Improved appearance (6) Security in old age (7) Praise from others (8) Comfort (9) Leisure (10) Pride of accomplishment (11) Advancement: business, social (12) Increased enjoyment (13) Self-confidence (14) Personal prestige.

They want to BE . . . (1) Good parents (2) Sociable, hospitable (3) Up-to-date (4) Creative (5) Proud of their possessions (6) Influential over others (7) Gregarious (8) Efficient (9) "First" in things (10) Recognized as authorities.

They want to DO . . . (1) Express their personalities (2) Resist domination by others (3) Satisfy their curiosity (4) Emulate the admirable (5) Appreciate beauty (6) Acquire or collect things (7) Win others' affection (8) Improve themselves generally.

They want to SAVE . . . (1) Time (2) Money (3) Work (4) Discomfort (5) Worry (6) Doubts (7) Risks (8) Personal embarrassment.

If you will tie up the *advantages* of your product with what people want to gain, be, do, and save, you will make them want to buy. And if you will check back now over the motivating forces just listed, you will realize that Napoleon was not merely being cynical when he said, "There are two motives to action: self-interest and fear."

Psychological Background Behind These Desires

Some time ago I overheard a conversation between two girls. At the end of it one of the girls finally remarked, "Well, I wouldn't want to be made to look like a fool. I'm not sure that I know the right thing to do in this case, and I wouldn't want to risk doing the wrong thing. If I did, I would be awfully embarrassed and people would think I didn't have any education or manners or anything. I'd never live it down."

I do not know what egregious error the young lady was shying away from; but, translating her general attitude into a copy appeal, I suppose it would come under the one sometimes referred to as personal prestige. But there were other overtones and undertones in the conversation, touching on pride, protection against embarrassment, popularity, self-consciousness, inferiority complex, desire for praise, and others. So I began to wonder about the *background* behind a specific copy appeal, for, obviously, this background covers a great deal more territory than the copy man may envisage or realize when he (as we do above) uses a very general term, covering only a word or two, to identify it.

For example, when we write copy based on the appeal of money, or health, or security, or popularity, what area are we actually traversing, as far as the thoughts and feelings of the *reader* are concerned? What selling arguments of ours will best dovetail with the mass attitude of the average person in relation to those particular appeals?

YOUR READER—THE PRODUCT OF HIS PAST

I decided that it might be helpful to writers of advertising copy for me to try to delve into the psychological background *behind* the advertising appeals which we usually designate by just a few words.

The result was somewhat of a montage in first person singular form—filled with bromides, clichés, undigested and predigested "personal philosophizing," vagaries, and wisps of beliefs. Inevitably it could not be otherwise, for the average human mind *is* a montage of hasty impressions, fuzzy generalities, bromidic wall-motto sentiments, self-justifications, and sentimentalities.

Yet, since these areas are truly so lacking in clear delineation, it is important that the copy man try to chart them. By doing so he may be able to propel his copy appeals more accurately and effectively. And, even though the viewpoint of each person on any given human desire or appeal may differ in some measure, yet each undoubtedly falls into a fairly general pattern.

So here are suggested the background attitudes behind ten of the more common copy appeals. They are not based upon scientific psychological study. They are simply an attempt to set down, in the average person's own words, some observations which try to convey a picture of at least my own impression of how he thinks and feels (mostly feels, of course) in relation to basic human desires.

MONEY AND BETTER JOB

I'm interested in making more money and getting a bigger job. I am tired of worrying all the time where the next dollar is coming from. I don't know where my money all goes to. Life seems merely a succession of bills—and worry about how to pay them.

In my job with the company, it's the same old seniority, dead men's shoes. My work isn't appreciated as it should be, and my bosses do not credit me with my full ability. I've got lots on the ball. There's plenty of good stuff inside me. And I'm as capable as others. But I never seem to get a break.

Lord knows I work hard enough! But our place is rife with favoritism. Those who ingratiate themselves with the boss seem to have all the luck.

And I'm sick of having people hint all the time about how well others are doing. Sure, nothing succeeds like success—those who have, get.

I'd even like to go into business for myself sometime. My children must have the means to go to college and to have a better chance in life than I had. I am fed up with the grind and will go nuts unless I can make more of my life. There must be some kind of easy *short-cut* to getting ahead faster.

I can't seem to lay anything by, or have enough to spend, or save, or to just give away if I feel like it. It isn't that I do not have ideas— I have lots of them and I think they are good. But other people seem to put theirs over and I just haven't been able to. But I'll show 'em. I'll turn the tables on them.

I don't want to take orders all the time. I want to *give* 'em—have some power over other people. But I won't cringe and knuckle down in order to push myself ahead. I just wouldn't stoop the way some people do. Of course, I've muffed a few good chances but it wasn't my fault.

I'm not really greedy about money. I don't care about being really rich, just comfortably well off. (This transparent disavowal reminds one of Abraham Lincoln's story about the farmer who said, "I ain't greedy about land. I only want what jines mine!")

SECURITY IN OLD AGE

I'm interested in security when I get older. I have worked hard all my life. When I get along in years I want to be able to take it easy. I don't want to be dependent on others. I want to hold my head up and not take any charity. I don't want to live on anybody. I want to do the things I've always dreamed about, go where I want, and not be worried all the time.

A person ought to be able to get away from the battle when he's older, and look on for a while, in safety and security. What's the use of battling every day unless you can have some peace and quiet to look forward to later.

There's a lot of things I've wanted to do all my life, but I've never had time or money to do them. What travel have I done? When I was a kid I dreamed of seeing the whole world. Year after year that hope was squeezed out of me. Before I could get going on any of my dreams the responsibilities piled up and kept my nose to the grindstone.

There must be some sure, safe way to become independent before you're too old to enjoy it.

POPULARITY

I'm interested in making myself more popular. It's fun to be asked out all the time, to be "wanted" by everyone. There's no fun being a wallflower. I'll never forget that wonderful chapter in Booth Tarkington's *Alice Adams* where Alice stood there for hours, praying for someone to pay some attention to her, to dance with her. It was enough to tear you apart.

Some people I know have their phone ringing all the time with invitations. I don't like to push myself forward for attention, but I suppose I am a little too self-conscious and inclined to stand in the background.

Sometimes I seem able to become quite the hit of the party. Some people I know seem to get asked all over because they flatter others. They haven't any better personality or more charm than I have, but I just won't be insincere in order to win a lot of attention.

I get so sick and tired sometimes of waiting for the phone to ring or hoping that the postman will bring me invitations. I've got lots of good points. I'm intelligent and not bad looking and I can talk interestingly—when I want to. But I guess I "hide my light under a bushel." Maybe I have an inferiority complex—but I really shouldn't because I'm not *really* inferior to other people who are always popular.

PRAISE FROM OTHERS

I'm interested in getting recognition from others for the qualities I know I have. I don't like flattery but there's no harm in having people tell you that you have intelligence, that the clothes you are wearing look attractive, that some of your possessions are obviously not inexpensive or that your choice of something indicates that you have good taste and good judgment.

There are some things that I think I'm even an authority on and it is nice when people recognize it. I like hearing it said that I am a good parent and have done a good job with my children. Of course, what I do for them I do for their sakes, but I can't deny that I like it when they reflect credit on me, too.

I don't mind hearing myself praised as being up-to-date. And anyone can see that I appreciate things that are cultural and beautiful, that I am creative and efficient, and that I am often in the lead and "first" in many things.

After all, I really do things well and I *have* overcome many obstacles and difficulties. Praise from others is a nice thing to get and I like to get it when I deserve it—and I often do.

MORE COMFORT

I'm interested in things that add to my comfort. I work pretty hard and have done so all my life. I deserve a little ease and luxury once in a while. You couldn't call it self-indulgence. It's just that I really rate some relief from work and inconvenience and worry once in a while.

I deserve more leisure, too—for travel, or hobbies, or rest, or play, or for self-development in some of the things that I have thought about so many times.

I am not pitying myself or putting up a hard-luck story. But I do know that a lot of people who are really not as industrious or capable as I am seem to have more comforts, more conveniences, and more freedom from a lot of the worries that beset me. So why shouldn't I spread myself once in a while?

SOCIAL ADVANCEMENT

I'm interested in moving up into better social circles. Not that I want to "keep up with the Joneses"—not showing off, but just advancing myself socially. There's nothing wrong with that, is there? Where would a person be if he never tried to better himself and to meet and associate with better people.

I'm certainly good enough. This is a democratic country and no one has to stay on the wrong side of the track. I could do myself credit in any circle that I know of. I'm not trying to be snooty but unless you try to push yourself forward, you are bound to go back.

I don't want to lose any chance I can get to meet and associate with the better people of this town and I'm going to think carefully about the groups I join. Also, I want my children to be able to mix with anyone. And if the head of the firm or anyone else important visits me or takes an interest in me I want to carry it through with credit.

IMPROVED APPEARANCE

I'm interested in improving my appearance. I don't expect crowds to thrill in rapture over me, but I do think that I'm not too plain and that I can really do things for myself that will make me even more attractive. Other people make a great deal of themselves, people who have less than I have to start with.

It's awfully nice to have people tell you how attractive and well dressed you are. It's everyone's job to make the most of himself. There's no such thing these days as the necessity of being homely. There are too many things to do about it.

Some people whose features are exceedingly commonplace have succeeded in becoming almost beautiful. No person has the right to fail to make himself more prepossessing to others. If I had the time and the money that some people spend on themselves—would I *show* them!

PERSONAL PRESTIGE

I'm interested in doing things right. There's nothing so embarrassing as making mistakes that cause other people to misjudge you and to consider you less educated or cultured than you really are. I may not have come from a blue-blood family but that doesn't mean that I don't know, or can't learn, how to do things properly.

Thank goodness, in this country you are not held back by any handicaps you've had in life. I just don't want to do or say anything that stamps me as not as good as the next one.

I can make up for whatever I have missed and I am going to see to it that my children can prove that they have parents they never need be ashamed of. Nobody is going to look down his nose at *me!* I don't ever want to give any offense to others. I want to hold up my head and keep my self-respect and not run any risks of making a fool of myself.

BETTER HEALTH

I'm interested in better health, and in strength, vigor and endurance. I used to feel wonderful all the time, but I don't know what's gotten into me lately. I suppose I don't take the best possible care of myself, but I just don't get time to be coddling myself all the time.

I am really not a "hypo," who is always complaining about nothing. Whenever I don't feel too well it is due to ailments that are not imaginary. I could do so much more if I felt marvelous all the time.

I am not really old and I don't feel any older than I did a year ago. It's just that I don't seem to have the drive and the energy I used to have. I've had a pretty strenuous time all my life and it's no wonder that it may be beginning to tell on me a little bit.

I just haven't thought enough about myself. I always seem to be thinking and considering other people and sort of letting myself go. People always tell me that I think of myself last. There must be lots of quick short-cuts for getting back the kind of health I used to have.

INCREASED ENJOYMENT

I'm interested in as much enjoyment as I can get from entertainment, food, drink, and other pleasures. You might as well live life to the full. You're only here once and you just can't take it with you.

After all, I work hard, I do the best I can about things, and I try to do what's right. So why shouldn't I get as much enjoyment as I can?

I'm not really thinking of myself all the time, but if I don't consider myself once in a while, who else will? So it is not being selfish for me to have things I will get some enjoyment out of.

Life is not so full of constant happiness that I should pass up things and sacrifice pleasures that will make up for some of the disappointments and troubles I have had.

A COMPOSITE "PORTRAIT" OF THE AVERAGE PERSON

And so it looks as though we have some sort of composite of the average human being—after having made an attempt to portray the background which he brings *to* your advertisement and which influences, favorably or unfavorably, his personal reaction to it. In this background portrait are some of the myriad variations and combinations of training, education, traits, feelings, superstitions, and "personal philosophizing" that make him up.

This undoubtedly oversimplified portrait may be at variance with your own conception of him. Your portrait may show him to be more commendable, more intelligent, more clear-cut in his attitudes; and less self-pitying, self-indulgent, self-seeking.

Perhaps, however, this delineation may help you to visualize your own concept of the average person to whom you are directing a specific appeal. For when you line up and send out a copy appeal, you are, of course, not shooting it into a void; you are projecting it directly against the general already-existent attitude of the average person—*as he has already thought of that particular appeal in relation to himself.* And your new message will either combat or concur with his own strongly held or partly jelled viewpoint.

People are more likely to agree with you if you first agree with them—by showing them that you have a sympathetic understanding of how they already feel. Your own composite portrait may be more heroic than this one, or it may be even more filled with human frailties. But it is a good thing to have such a portrait in your mind when you are trying to move the average person into action.

New Trends for Old

Now that we've finished our attempt at a dissection of the average individual, it is likewise beneficial for the copywriter to know the broad social trends which have a bearing upon his work.

To help you do this I have condensed and paraphrased a lengthy statement I once read. It was written by a sociologist—and it does not, unfortunately, portray a more heroic picture of the trends of mass psychology than we have already painted of the individual's.

Briefly, and broadly speaking, I think that the general trend of our times seems toward a preference for:

Success	—instead of—	Integrity
Spending	—instead of—	Saving
Restlessness	—instead of—	Rest
Self-Indulgence	—instead of—	Self-Discipline
Desire for the New or Novel	—instead of—	Affection for the Old and Tried
Show	—instead of—	Solidity
Dependence	—instead of—	Self-Reliance
Gregariousness	—instead of—	Solitude
Luxury	—instead of—	Simplicity
Ostentation	—instead of—	Restraint
Easy Generosity	—instead of—	Wise Giving
Quick Impressions	—instead of—	Careful Thought

Like it or not, these are trends which the thoughtful copywriter must consider when writing copy based upon a mass appeal—despite, happily, the many commendable human desires and appeals previously discussed. And, to those people with enough years of observation of the human race behind them, there is obviously sufficient validity to these trends to justify their inclusion in the copywriter's frame of reference.

HOW SHALL WE SELECT OUR COPY APPEAL?

Now which advantage (or advantages) are you going to feature in your copy, in your illustration, or perhaps in both? Which appeal, based on a human desire, will move people most naturally and surely toward your product? How will you present it most dramatically, convincingly?

To be a keen judge of appeals, and to present them well in copy and illustration, you have to become "people," not merely remain a "person." To show people an advantage you've got to *be* people, to have within you the distilled essence of their feelings, desires, emotions, and thoughts. The advice of Horace, the Roman poet, to writers was that *they* must weep first if they wished to make their audiences weep.

So don't get out of touch with the thinking and feeling of ordinary, average people. Remember that the more successful an advertising man becomes, the more he risks the influence of what Hal Stebbins calls "country-club thinking"—and the loss of his down-to-earth understanding of the very people whose mass response to his work has *made* him successful. He has to be able to "walk with Kings —nor lose the common touch."

William I. Nicholas, managing editor of *This Week,* put it this way:

It is very nice to be an executive, but on the other hand, to the very extent that you climb up in your job, you tend to leave behind you the people on whom all power, influence and success depend. It is like climbing a mountain. As you go up and pass the timber line, the fog rolls in and you lose sight of the valley down below. . . . If you are not careful you will forget those plain people from whom all your strength must come. If you are not very careful, you lose the wave length that goes into their lives and thoughts. And if that happens, then all the tricks, all the reader surveys, all the typographical devices in the world will be of no avail.

Carrying this thought a step further, Mark O'Dea once wrote: "To know the mass mind is no simple matter—to interpret what to do when one learns it is a greater problem. The inclination of an advertiser or writer who lives a conservative life is to be conservative in addressing others, possibly using an intellectual approach, whereas his audience can be moved only by the emotions."

As a writer of advertising you are, as I have said, no longer merely a person, one who is influenced by your own individual ideas or the reactions and copy opinions of your wife or your own immediate circle of friends. In fact, three of the most expensive words in advertising are perhaps "My wife says . . ."!

If you pay much attention to such reactions you are likely to be doubly misled: qualitatively, because they are probably not representative of the mass-market mind; and quantitatively because (even regardless of that) there are not enough of them to give an accurate sample. For example, statisticians have figured—using the law of probability—that a 100-vote poll would probably be 20 per cent wrong; 1,000 votes, 6 per cent; 50,000, 1 per cent. The error grows smaller, of course, as the number of ballots mounts.

Meaning no disrespect to the American consumer (one of whom I am proud to be), the advertising man must always keep in front of his mind and his typewriter the old adage, "It's not the taste of the angler that counts: it's the taste of the *fish*."

Failure to observe this familiar aphorism sometimes leads an advertiser to "over-Ritz" the advertising of his product. His pride seeks to give it glamour (as he views it), whereas his customers can be moved more effectively by an appeal to economy or some other unromantic factor.

Judy O'Grady and the Colonel's Lady

Yet, as Kipling tells us, "the colonel's lady and Judy O'Grady are sisters under their skins." What application has this to advertising copy? A very close one . . . but frequently ignored.

For example, perhaps you can recall some advertisement of a "quality" product, addressed to the colonels or the colonels' ladies of civilian life. It pulls its punches. It is delicately reticent, obsequiously shy about stressing the reasons why you should buy the product. It is so fearful of seeming importunate that it neglects to mention many strong selling points.

So? Are the purchasers of quality products easier to sell than those who are in more "Judy O'Grady" circumstances? Hardly. On the contrary, people who are more affluent are usually the more careful buyers, need even more facts and persuasion than those who are a cut below in the social scale. For example, do you know what surveys tell us about the redemption of those little grocery-product coupons, worth only 5 cents, 10 cents, or 15 cents each? Low-income families produce the *lowest* percentage of the redemption which would entitle them to make these savings!

Yes, advertising which does not get under this epidermis of position or circumstance, which does not get down to the most basic human appeals and motivations, misses a lot of people—and sales. For, obviously, no reader can be influenced by good sales angles which don't appear in the advertisement at all!

Do you recall the old story of the man who lost his horse and who found him so quickly? He was asked how he knew exactly where to look and he answered, "I just said to myself, if I were a horse where would I go? I went there and there he was."

To become a keener judge of advertising appeals avoid getting out of touch with the thinking and feeling of ordinary, average people. Here are five ways to do it:

1. *Read* . . . the comics, newspaper, and magazine features, stories and books which have the largest popular following. Also read the truly great books which bring ordinary people to life before your eyes and make you understand them.
2. *See* . . . the smash-hit movies, television shows, and plays whose entertainment values attract millions of people.
3. *Listen* . . . to those particular radio programs which hold the interest of countless people week after week.
4. *Talk* . . . with taxi drivers, laborers, newsboys, clerks, and others who do not inhabit the more rarefied social and economic heights.
5. *Study* . . . the appeals and the copy of the mail-order advertisements which continue to repeat their mass-market messages, because they aren't repeated unless they pay in direct, checkable results.

Eliminating the "Testing of the Obvious"

To learn more and more about "what makes people tick" will help you in another way. It can guide you toward eliminating, safely, at least some of the "preliminary testing" that costs time and money. It can cut down that all-too-common and expensive "testing of the obvious" which, at the end, merely reiterates superfluous confirmation of already known and proved principles of why people react as they do, and just what stimuli make them do so.

Of course, copy tests are very often required, and they can and do isolate effective copy appeals on a given product. But an advertising man who really "knows *people*" also usually acquires a dependable intuition based on this knowledge. And, although not infallible, he is infinitely better able to judge more accurately beforehand the instances in which a test is absolutely necessary . . . and those in which the resultant human reaction to a certain appeal, when presented in a certain way, is so palpably inevitable (or at least so extremely and fundamentally probable) that the exhaustive and costly testing of it may safely be eliminated.

Now, as Aesop Glim says, "The arresting power of an advertisement is the ability of the main illustration, the headline and the layout—as a composite unit—*to force a reading of the first paragraph* by those who are your prospects."

That first paragraph is vital—and the literature of advertising has not stressed that point sufficiently. So let us do so now.

IMPORTANCE OF YOUR FIRST PARAGRAPH

This chapter about the second fundamental in the writing of a good advertisement (*Show People an Advantage*) of course relates to the body copy you use in presenting your sales appeals. However, the vital determinant of whether your reader will get to *reading* that copy is a subject about which too little has ever been written in the literature of advertising: your first paragraph.

"A good headline," said Howard Newton, of J. M. Mathes, Inc., "gets your foot in the door of the reader's mind. An unfortunate lead paragraph can cause you to lose a couple of toes." Actually, your first paragraph can, *in itself,* determine whether or not the reader will continue reading your ad at all. Briefly stated, it should:

Follow through with the idea or appeal expressed in the main headline—which is what attracted the reader in the first place.

Be short, with quick, easy-to-read sentences; entice the reader to stay with you into the paragraphs which follow.

Perhaps start with a question, one so pertinent or challenging as to grip the reader's interest at once and impel him to keep reading to find the answer.

Start immediately to carry out the reward-for-reading promise made in your headline. Compress into this paragraph a few of the major advantages of your product. Don't clutter it up with minor claims. In the words of Jim Young, "There are many ways to start an ad, but one of the best, if not *the* best, is to tell the reader how to get something he already wants. The formula is simple enough, but the real problem is to put your finger on that want. It may be something so obvious—like the merchandise itself—that you will tend to overlook it, and start farther back than you need to."

Two Examples—One Bad

Here are two examples of first paragraphs. The first one is the lead in an unsuccessful advertisement selling etchings, the other in a successful one.

A group of America's foremost artists have agreed to permit a *limited sale* of their own personally-signed original Etchings and Lithographs, at only a fraction of the price that their work of equal museum-quality regularly commands!

What exquisite new loveliness and charm these Signed Originals will add to your home! Nothing else you could place on your walls is in such perfect taste, so sure a touch of refinement. Your guests will admire these Originals tremendously. And they will never dream you obtained them for only $5 each—because their normal value ranges from $18 to $36.

What a difference! No. 1 tells what the *advertiser* is doing. No. 2 tells what the product is going to do for *you*.

THEY'LL GO SO FAR AND NO FARTHER—UNLESS . . .

Your first paragraph is usually the most difficult to write. And it often happens that writing your first few paragraphs has simply been a warm-up exercise. So you discard those and start the ad with your next one.

Remember that your readers will not go far along with you unless your first paragraph holds the attention and interest which your headline and layout have aroused. So this is a vital step in the successful accomplishment of your entire objective. For, as explained in Chapter 6, the *longer* your copy can hold the interest of the greatest number of readers, the likelier you are to induce *more* of them to act.

This chapter on how to *Show People an Advantage* naturally stresses appeals to the emotions and instincts, the primary motivating forces. But, as James D. Woolf said, "The size of the promise determines the power of the pull—*and the promise had better stick, or else.*"

So the next chapter (*Prove It*) will stress those elements in an advertisement which, in the main, become appeals to reason. And that means the presentation of the kind of factual evidence which not only proves your claims of what your product will *do* for people but which also provides people with sound reasons to indicate (or, if questioned, to vindicate) their good judgment—in case their emotions get the better of them and they fall headlong into the pit of a purchase.

QUIZ ON CHAPTER 2

1. What do people want to know about a product, above everything else?

2. Why should you be "on both sides of the counter"?

3. Name six of the twelve *major* desires which motivate people.

4. What is meant by "country-club thinking"?

5. Is it easier to sell to Judy O'Grady than to the colonel's lady?

6. Which five things can you do to become a keener judge of advertising appeals?

7. How can the "testing of the obvious" be cut down?

8. Why is the first paragraph of your copy so vital?

9. What should it do?

10. Why does this chapter stress the appeals to the emotions and instincts?

TELL ME QUICK AND TELL ME TRUE
(OR ELSE, MY LOVE, TO HELL WITH YOU!)

("I turn over page after page of the magazines, costing the advertisers thousands per page; and *still* they are talking about themselves and—as far as I am concerned—to themselves." Comment by a reader.)

I see that you've spent quite a big wad of dough
To tell me the things *you* think I should know.
How your plant is so big, so fine, and so strong;
And your founder had whiskers so handsomely long.

So he started the business in old '92!
How tremendously int'resting *that* is . . . to you.
He built up the thing with the blood of his life?
(I'll run home like mad, tell that to my wife!)

Your machinery's modern and oh
so complete;
Your "rep" is so flawless; your
workers so neat.
Your motto is "Quality" . . . capi-
tal "Q"—
No wonder I'm tired of "Your"
and of "You"!

So tell me quick and tell me true
(Or else, my love, to hell with
you!)
Less—"how this product came to
be";
More—what the damn thing does
for *me!*

Will it save me money or time or
work;
Or hike up my pay with a welcome
jerk?
What drudgery, worry, or loss will
it cut?
Can it yank me out of a personal
rut?

Perhaps it can make my appearance so swell
That my telephone calls will wear
out the bell;
And thus it might win me a lot of
fine friends—
(And one never knows where *such*
a thing ends!)

I wonder how much it could do
for my health?
Could it show me a way to acquire
some wealth—
Better things for myself, for the
kids and the wife,
Or how to quit work somewhat
early in life?

So tell me quick and tell me true
(Or else, my love, to hell with
you!)
Less—"how this product came to
be";
More—what the damn thing does
for *me!*

A bit of doggerel written in 1942 which summarizes some of the
suggestions just mentioned in Chapter 2. By using the word "quick"
in these verses I do not mean (as many readers over the years have
mistakenly supposed) that the copy has to be *short*. I simply mean
that its principal appeals be presented quickly in the headline and/or
the body copy.

———————

CHAPTER 3

PROVE IT

When, in the preceding chapter, we were discussing our second fundamental, *Show People an Advantage,* we found that the way to do it was to stress appeals to the emotions and instincts, the primary motivating forces. But this is not enough. The body of a sale comprises both flesh and bone, the flesh of an emotional response and the hard bone of fact to support it.

Now, although *Prove It* is the third of our five fundamentals, it of course does *not* mean that "proof material" must be presented in this same sequence in the actual preparation of an advertisement. (That is true of other of our fundamentals. For example, the best headline may pop out during your writing of the body copy itself.) So "proof material" may be used throughout the whole advertisement. It may even be used as headline and display material, particularly when it has dramatic attention-getting value or when it, in itself, demonstrates what the product will do for people.

In the latter case the copy becomes inductive: the proof material comes first and the assertions of resultant advantages come afterward, whereas the more commonly used (and more generally applicable) *deductive* copy begins with assertions of advantages and then backs up the claims with proof.

Why You Need Facts—and Where

However, especially in connection with this third fundamental, *Prove It,* the statement of Professor Albert T. Poffenberger, in his

Psychology in Advertising, should be kept in mind: "The processes involved in the human reaction to an advertisement are too complex and too much interwoven with each other to permit of analysis into a chain of distinct and loosely connected operations, each to be examined in isolation from all the others." It is therefore obvious that proof material may be introduced into any part of the advertisement, from headline to close.

Why are facts so necessary? You need them in order to create and justify conviction; and you need conviction in order to create and justify sales. Dr. Charles M. Edwards, professor in the Graduate School of Retailing at New York University, once stated: "The more facts you tell, the more you sell. An advertisement's chance for success invariably increases as the number of pertinent merchandise *facts* included in the advertisement increases."

TWO OF THE REASONS

Here are two of the reasons why it is so necessary to work plenty of "prove it" facts into your advertisement—and to review your copy thoroughly to make sure that you have done so:

First, for the very general reason that people probably discount all advertising claims just as seriously these days as they ever did before. Far too many of them wonder whether the philosophy of advertisers is not similiar to that of Mark Twain's Puddinhead Wilson, who said: "Tell the truth or trump—but get the trick." In fact, one of Daniel Starch's investigations indicated that almost 80 per cent of those who read 342 of the advertisements of leading national advertisers questioned the veracity of these advertisements. The more facts you present, the more credible your advertisement, and everything in it, will become.

Second, and more specifically: People need facts and want facts as reasons *and* excuses for buying—in order to justify to themselves (and to others) a decision which may be based on their emotions alone.

This is a very important point. So perhaps it might be well to emphasize it by quoting a statement by Clyde Bedell from *How to Write Advertising That Sells:*

> The head certainly can't go along and concur with the heart without some reasons. Now all this process is one of rationalization. To rationalize is to bring props of reason to support decisions arrived at emotionally. The skilled copy writer attempts to provide the reader of advertising with a basis for rationalization. In short, the real advertising writer who is after results makes the reader want something—and then provides what the reader will consider a good excuse for buying it.

Two Forces Are Needed to Pull a Sale

The above quotation makes it clear how emotion (No. 2, *Show People an Advantage*) and reason (No. 3, *Prove It*) work together in an advertisement to produce a sale. Now let's summarize some of the things each does for the other:

Your No. 3 proof-material copy builds belief. It furnishes evidence of the advantages you have promised. It makes the reader feel that his purchase of the product will be safe and wise; that it will indicate his good judgment, and vindicate it, too, if that becomes necessary. He can't justify himself if he acts on emotion only. He has to have reasons. Your No. 3 copy gives him the kind of facts referred to by the philosopher William James when he said: "Our reason is quite satisfied, in nine hundred and ninety-nine cases out of every thousand of us, if it can find a few arguments that will do to recite in case our credulity is criticized by someone else."

And now, just how does your No. 2 appeal-to-emotion copy actually help your No. 3 appeal-to-reason copy? At first thought it may not seem that emotion can do much to back up reason. But it can and does. And here is why: The more strongly and effectively the emotional appeal is presented, the more fully and readily will your proof material be accepted and believed.

Never Forget This Psychological Truth

The above is a highly important psychological truth which has been brought out by many authorities. To clarify and emphasize the point let me quote three of them: "There can be no question," says Joseph Jastrow, in *The Psychology of Conviction,* "where beginnings lie. The original source of conviction is emotion." David Seabury, the psychologist, puts it this way: "Reason is powerless to change consciousness save when merged with emotion."

And here, concerning this truth, are a few passages from the book by Professor Poffenberger:

> Belief is a matter of feeling and emotion rather than of reason. . . . We tend to believe what arouses our desires, our fears, and our other emotions. . . . Once a belief has been established in this way, logic and reasoning may be used to support it. We may summarize these opinions concerning belief or conviction about as follows:
>
> 1. Belief is a matter of feeling and emotion rather than of reason.
> 2. The truth is not a primary factor in determining belief.
> 3. Belief is a personal matter, a fabric of *personal* experiences.
> 4. Belief has also a social component to be accounted for by the need for conformity with one's fellows and especially with those in authority.
> 5. Belief is dependent upon desire—*we believe what we want to believe.*

The Heart Dictates to the Head

Your reader *wants* to believe an ad if the appeal sounds good to him. The more effectively you present your No. 2 emotional factors, the more predisposed your reader becomes to believe the facts you present to justify your claims of consumer advantages.

Many advertisements filled with good emotional-appeal copy fail because they do not contain any, or enough, "prove it" facts to carry conviction. Likewise, many advertisements filled with good proof material fail because their emotional-appeal copy is not strong enough to motivate the reader to act. Both factors are needed, for one helps the other along the road toward the goal of action.

The French philosopher, Pascal, tells us that "The heart has its reasons with which reason is unacquainted"—and it has a great deal to do with dictating to the head what to believe . . . and even more about what to do about it. I once read a joke which exemplifies this point very well. The main job of a district manager for a vacuum cleaner company was hiring men and training them. To help a new man become familiar with the product, he suggested that he demonstrate it to his wife. The next morning he asked the new man how he got along.

"I did what you told me," he said. "And when I finished, I asked my wife, 'Would you buy it?' She said, 'Yes.' Then I asked her, 'Why?' She replied, 'Because I love you!' "

FIRST GET THE FACTS

Copy jobs are often tackled in a way which reminds one of that old wisecrack, "So he dashed out of the house, jumped on his horse, and galloped off in all directions." Good copy involves digging for facts before a word is written, not whirling around to a typewriter keyboard, and starting to bang out words.

Schopenhauer says, "There are three kinds of authors. First come those who write without thinking. . . . Then come those who do their own thinking while they are writing. . . . Last of all come those authors who think before they begin to write. They are rare." Which kind of copywriter are you?

It is surprising what a careful search for facts and figures can bring to the surface, on any commodity or service. Every product, new or old, has unsuspected or unexploited angles in it. Market research, for example, brings out many concrete facts which the copywriter may present imaginatively and convincingly. The merits and claims made for competitors' products, when studied thoroughly, can often lead to the discovery of superiorities and advantages in your own product.

And, entirely unavailable to competitors, the advertiser's own sales records and correspondence usually contain an arsenal of ammunition of known power in the battle for better advertising, greater sales volume, broader markets. Yet how frequently he turns to external sources for information . . . while his own files are crammed with priceless guidance!

Study your product, and everything that goes into it. Some of the specific things to look for will be suggested later. But if you will really dredge, you will find plenty of "prove it" facts about any product, regardless of what it may be.

Remember, Huxley wrote a very long factual essay about a little piece of chalk. Fabre wrote long books about the fly and the spider. In Matthew Josephson's book *Zola and His Time* appears this very interesting observation.

The thing to do is to examine everything you wish to express long enough and with enough attention to discover in it an aspect that no one else has ever seen or spoken of. There is something of the unexplored in everything, because we are accustomed to employing our eyes only with the memory of what has been thought before about the object of our contemplation. The very least object contains a little of the unknown. Let us look for it.

The Kind of Facts to Get

As mentioned in Chapter 1, newspaper writers have a saying, "Start where the reader is." This is a good thing to remember in your presentation of the facts to substantiate your claims. Find some common meeting ground. Whenever possible, get your reader's yes with familiar facts, and then you can more easily carry him on from the known to the unknown.

As Professor Poffenberger states, "Belief is a fabric of *personal* experiences." Therefore, among your facts, try to introduce a few which are likely to come within that experience. If you can do that your reader's reaction will be: "Yes, I *know* that, so I guess these other facts are true." The use of familiar facts helps to create belief, even though the reader may not be able to substantiate, out of his own personal experiences, all of the reasoning offered in the advertisement.

Now, what kinds of facts may be used as proof material—the proof of what your product will do for people. The following is my amplified version of those listed by the late G. B. Hotchkiss.

I. CONSTRUCTION EVIDENCE includes any facts about materials and manufacture of the product. Specifications of quality concerning ingredients, design, and details of workmanship *in the product itself*.

To itemize them more specifically:

A. Reputation and Standing as a Firm

How long in business, size—resources of plant, laboratory, finance, and other inanimate facilities—company policies indicative of its integrity, experience, and reputation—geographic, climatic, or other advantages of location which have a favorable bearing upon the merit and value of the product or service being sold.

B. Management Personnel

The accepted abilities and authoritative experience of the founder of the business—or of any of the executives responsible for its management.

C. Production or Service Personnel

Facts about the long-experienced craftsmen, engineers, research people, dietitians, stylists, designers, or workers who personally plan or turn out the product—or about those who install or service it.

D. Quality of Materials or Design

Laboratory-test facts, or other specifications, about tensile strength, streamline design, or any other elements attesting to durability, beauty, washability, utility, color fastness, purity, or any merit claimed for the product—the known and commonly accepted value of any one single ingredient used in the product may also be stressed particularly, thus carrying a greater share of the burden of proof. (This may even involve giving a new trade name to this single ingredient, to point up its specific effectiveness)—facts about who supplies various parts of the product, when the names of such suppliers have known sales value.

E. Patents or Machinery

Special processes or precision machinery, the use of which helps to back up claims of consumer benefits.

F. Speed of Delivery

Proving freshness, for example.

G. Design or Material *of Container*

Proving speed, handiness, and convenience when used; cleanliness, freshness, extra utility, reusability (perhaps for another purpose), etc.

II. PERFORMANCE EVIDENCE includes the achievements of the product *in actual use*. For example:

A. Achievements of Product

Endurance runs, mileage records, laundry tests, etc. Dramatic performance records—in either ordinary or unusually difficult conditions, such as arctic cold or tropical heat. True and believable before-and-after photographs.

B. Discriminating or Well-Known Users

Experience cited by advertiser, not in form of testimonials by users themselves, including proof of the advantages offered by the product to those to whom it has *exceptional* personal usefulness and necessity—such as foot-ease powder for policemen or postmen, watches for railroad men, or sunburn creams for life guards, etc.—or stressing the product as one which authorities themselves buy: for example, the cigarettes which tobacco experts smoke, the automobile which automotive engineers buy, the dentifrice which dentists use, etc.

C. Increasing Popularity

"Success talk"—constantly increasing sales figures.

D. "Demonstration" Reasons

Usually of a scientific or mechanical nature, clearly explaining how and why the product can and will bring the advantages claimed.

III. TESTIMONY OF OTHERS

Commendations, such as:

A. Performance evidence in the form of letters, statements, or records of the experience of *typical* actual users.

Baron Rothschild, the great banker, was once asked to make a business loan. "It's a sound loan," he replied. "Yet present plans won't permit me to lend you the money. But I will walk with you across the Exchange floor." He did—and the loan was at once made by another banker who saw them together. The baron's mere gesture was a sufficient testimonial to the integrity of the borrower. "Who says what" about your product can make strong advertising copy. What *you* say is naturally subject to a certain amount of discount by the reader. Who supports your claims?

The "dead storage" files of many an advertiser bulge with sincere, unsolicited, gratuitous endorsements—crammed with the most effective copy of all: the enthusiastic "here's what happened" case-history reports of those whose true experience with the product would carry more selling power than anything the advertiser himself might ever have the temerity to claim for it.

B. Expert Evidence

The statements of analytical and exacting authorities (such as scientists, engineers, physicians, dietitians, etc.) who commend, or use, the product.

C. Awards or Contests Won

Official recognition won in races, contests, expositions, laboratory tests; records broken, etc.—perhaps against competitive products.

D. Significant Outlets Selling Product Successfully

Sales records showing constantly increasing popularity and consumer demand. Facts or figures proving consumer satisfaction. Discriminating outlets with a reputation for carrying quality merchandise—who stock the product and sell it successfully.

IV. TEST EVIDENCE

A. A guarantee demonstrating the manufacturer's willingness to allow the quality of the product to speak for itself.

B. Free Sample

The mere willingness to supply this proof may be a strong factor in stimulating actual purchase of product rather than mere acceptance of a sample.

The Missing Ingredient in Many an Otherwise Good Advertisement

It has already been said that the "dead storage" files of many advertisers bulge with persuasive facts sent to them by users of their products. Yet how frequently we see otherwise good advertisements which could be made even more powerful by the use of strong "who says what" testimonials. As James W. Young says in his *Diary of an Ad Man:* "Every type of advertiser has the same problem; namely, to be believed. The mail-order man knows nothing so potent for this purpose as the testimonial, yet the general advertiser seldom uses it."

Also, when testimonials *are* used, they are often ones which exhibit what one might call a kind of "transparenthusiasm." Their enthusiasm is transparent. They sound artificial, forced, as though "written to order" and using phrases similar to those which appear in the advertisement itself. When cutting the wordage in a testimonial (which is usually necessary), retain the sincerity and humanness of it, the perhaps awkward grammar, the colloquialism, the layman's idiom. And use the full name and address (and photograph, if possible) of its writer, if you have obtained full written permission to do so.

USE "PROVE IT" FACTS THAT ARE FULLY CREDIBLE

History tells us that the age-old customs of mankind include one involving the hiring of "professional mourners" to eulogize the deceased and to inject considerable artistry into the lamentations for his passing. It is entirely natural for us to discount the sincerity of these hired hands. Now copywriters are, in effect, "professional enthusiasts", so it is likewise natural for readers of advertisements to discount the claims made in them.

How great that discount will be is determined by the extent and inherent believability of the claims made in your advertisement, whether you introduce facts to prove these claims, and how credible these facts are to the average reader. Obviously, facts which are incredible prove nothing; an advertisement which arouses nothing but disbelief is an expense, not an investment. In this chapter we have already discussed the kind of facts which may be used as credible proof material. Here, however, are a few ways to add to their credibility:

1. Use statements that also *ring* true. Sometimes actual truth may be so startling as to seem unbelievable. Instead of bucking the tide of utter disbelief, it may be wiser to tone it down by understanding the truth. As James D. Woolf, the advertising consultant, says: "We have faith in a promised benefit only as long as there is nothing in our experience to dispute or contradict it."

2. People are satiated with claims of perfection. Understatement can carry more conviction than palpable overstatement. Credibility for *all* the claims made is increased when relatively minor faults are admitted. Bernice Fitz-Gibbon cites an example:

> A little bad makes the good believable. A recent automobile campaign admitted frankly that cars that cost much more had better

upholstery and finer appointments. This was smart selling. In the first place, everybody knows that it's true. And the easiest way to make a person believe what you are going to tell him is first to tell him something that he already knows is true.

3. To make your facts more convincing, make them specific. 99 44/100% pure. (Not 100% perfect.) 48.5% above government specifications. (Not "almost 50%.") 989,000 of these pens have already been sold. (Not "almost one million.")

4. The use of actual photographs, rather than drawings, increases credibility. Split-run tests have been made in which an advertisement containing a photograph outpulled by a high percentage the very same one containing a drawing.

5. Get more "why" into it. Believability is increased if stark claims are substantiated by clear, reasonable, and logical copy about *why* the promise can be performed. Even a "miracle" consumer benefit is credible if the "why" of it is well presented.

How to Present *Your Facts*

Specific facts such as these will help you to prove your claims about what your product will do for people. But equally important is a knowledge of how to present these facts. Here are some quick pointers which are worth remembering:

Dramatize Your Facts. One example is the advertising of a well-known flashlight battery which showed dramatically, in words and pictures, why and how the dependability of the product saved lives in emergencies.

Present Your Facts from the Consumer's Point of View—not from the manufacturer's. Technical specifications should be translated into the kind of human-interest proof material that illustrates clearly and interestingly what the presence of these intrinsic qualities will do for the reader.

Be Specific. Give details. Where were the product tests made?

When? How? Where do the ingredients of the product come from?

Localize Your Testimonial Material Whenever Possible. When you are using a newspaper, the commendations of local people (with photographs and full name and address, if you can get releases) mean more than commendations of people in an entirely different section of the country.

Use "Performance Evidence" When You Can. It is usually more effective than "construction evidence" because it shows the average buyer what the product has actually done, rather than merely what it was built to do.

If a Reduced Price Is a Fact Give a Good Reason for It. The reason for a cut in price (particularly for an unexpectedly low one) is as important as the price itself. Do you remember a certain well-known series of advertisements offering oriental rugs at a greatly reduced price? The reasons given were interesting and convincing—telling how the wholesale buyer's experiences in the bazaars of the Orient had made possible his exceptionally advantageous purchases.

Now to sum up the three fundamentals discussed so far: First, *Get Attention.* Second, *Show People an Advantage.* Third, *Prove It.* In the next chapter (No. 4—*Persuade People to GRASP This Advantage*) will be given suggestions on how to weave your claims of benefits, and the facts to prove them, into convincing "closing-talk" copy.

QUIZ ON CHAPTER 3

1. Can "prove it" material be presented *anywhere* in an advertisement?

2. Give two reasons why the proof of your claims should be presented.

3. Why, strangely enough, does appeal-to-reason copy actually increase the persuasiveness of appeal-to-emotion copy?

4. Name some of the kinds of facts you should use to support the claims your copy makes.

5. There is one often-overlooked place which sometimes contains a gold mine of good proof material. Where is it?

6. What is the difference between "construction evidence" and "performance evidence"?

7. Which is the missing ingredient in many otherwise good advertisements?

8. Why is it sometimes advisable to tone down the actual truth?

9. Recall to yourself the example given of the dramatization of a fact.

10. Why is it better to present your facts from the consumer's point of view, rather than from the manufacturer's?

———

TOO MUCH SAND

Spinach isn't the only thing that can have too much sand in it. There's concrete, for instance, and advertising careers.

Let's talk about concrete first. That brings up the life of Joe, a stonemason I know who lives in a little upstate town. Joe is about seventy now, I guess. For fifty of those years he's been a stonemason. Not for the native folk; mostly for city people who come up for two or three months in summer and for a winter weekend occasionally.

Joe still is hale and hearty. Ready to do any stone work that comes his way. But none does—and he wonders why. He knows that there is a lot of summer-home building going on. So he broods about it quite a bit. And to feed his still husky frame he goes around peddling little pottery gimcracks that he makes.

However, that's not the tragedy of it. He still eats, and he never did want to work too hard anyway. Well, what's all the shooting for, then?

Just this. When you or I think of the idea of building a stone fence, we like to think of creating a fine solid work of masonry that would outlast Joe a generation or two. Or a chimney that will always stand up straight and firm and true. Or a fireplace that will pour out its glow and its warmth for as many years as any family is there to cluster around it. Or a terrace that can laugh at the rompings of an elephant.

But with Joe, no. Every year something that Joe has sometime made crumbles or cracks or falls. Sections of his stone fences fall down. His chimneys settle, sag, get out of plumb. His fireplaces develop seams and faulty draughts. His terraces all too soon are worried at the rompings of even little children. It seems every single job he ever did will sometime have to be done over.

And the natives of the town have a funny feeling that somehow Joe has done something awfully wrong with his life. Something even kind of tragically wrong, too, when they think about it a bit. But they're not as handy with words as advertising men are. So the way they put it is simply: "That stubborn mule, Joe. All these years we've told him time and again that he always put too much sand in his cement!"

I guess advertising careers have too much sand in them, too. Over the years we can all regretfully look back on many jobs we've done which came out straight run-of-the-mill. We just didn't put enough cement into them to make them hold together too well or too long. Of course, we're all a lot more rushed and harried and top-level pestered than Joe ever was. That can bring a fellow's batting average down pretty badly. And we know that nobody can knock 'em cold on every job he tackles. Even Homer nodded, and Shakespeare sometimes dozed.

It's just a matter, I suppose, of trying right along to get a better ratio between the sand and the cement. Less filler and more binder. More of the kind of copy jobs, for example, that have so much good work in them that they move people and goods. More of the type of superior research job whose basic soundness will stand up under any assault. More of the kind of space buying and time buying that is based on schedules that are built carefully and analytically.

In other words, more of the kind of above-the-average work in any branch of advertising that will better accomplish the fundamental chore of our business: to get into the hands of as many people as possible a piece of merchandise or a service which, at a fair price, does such a worth-while job that people will be glad they bought it.

That's a big order for us advertising people. We can't deliver it every day, or perhaps not even every week or month—at least not in the exceptional quality I'm thinking of. But we can all try to deliver it more often. Joe didn't even try to deliver it at all.

———————

CHAPTER 4

PERSUADE PEOPLE TO GRASP
THIS ADVANTAGE

This important Fundamental No. 4 is usually either completely ignored or underestimated by the preceptors of advertising *and* its practitioners.

When you get to this point in the writing of an advertisement you are near the end of the line. You have gained attention with your headline and layout. (Fundamental No. 1.) You have held interest by showing advantages. (Fundamental No. 2.) You have proved that your product can deliver these advantages. (Fundamental No. 3.) You will soon *Ask for Action* (Fundamental No. 5.)

So now (Fundamental No. 4) you motivate these benefits even more definitely than you may already have done earlier in the advertisement. You put wheels under them. You picture the benefits in actual motion in the daily lives of the people reading your copy. You sum up your Sales story. You paint a quick and summarized mind's-eye portrait of what the product will do for your reader, and how easy it is for him to get it.

This clincher copy may, in a shorter advertisement, represent only one or two sentences. In longer copy it may represent several paragraphs. But in either case it is a final setting of the stage preparatory to asking for some specific action on the part of the reader. It gathers up various threads of claims and proof; weaves them into a strong close. It reiterates. It reminds. It sums up.

A $600,000,000 Example

Back in 1900, J. P. Morgan and the greatest money masters of steel (with the exception of Andrew Carnegie) sat at a banquet table. Those present at the dinner already knew that a merger with Carnegie would bring them all tremendous advantages, in power and profit. They had realized it for a long time. But the speech Charles M. Schwab made that evening spurred them to positive and immediate action, and started them into motion toward grasping these advantages.

Schwab's speech put wheels under the latent desires of these assembled millionaires. Their next move was to get together, appoint him as their representative, and authorize him to see if Carnegie could not be induced to agree to a merger. Schwab accepted the assignment. He persuaded Carnegie to grasp an advantage which had long also appealed to *him:* retirement in comfort, with time and millions to devote to his many public benefactions.

This story of a $600,000,000 bit of persuasion will help to illustrate our fourth fundamental. Every person concerned in this gigantic deal already knew of the advantages (Fundamental No. 2) which would accrue to him and to his firm through a merger of the tremendous steel interests involved. Each person was fully convinced (Fundamental No. 3) of the desirability of this merger. And Charles M. Schwab personifies for us the *additional* motivation necessary to stimulate positive action toward the grasping of these advantages (Fundamental No. 4).

A Simple Illustration of It in Action

Suppose you are writing a piece of copy about a suit of clothes for a man. Your copy may first have pointed out how well your reader will look in it, how well it will fit him, why its quality represents a wise purchase. In other words, you have shown him certain advantages and you have proved them.

Now, to go further in persuading him to *grasp* these advantages, you may stress the benefits of the product in *use*. You may close by explaining that this is the kind of suit which assures him of the well-groomed appearance indicative of success, so necessary to those desirous of business or social advancement.

I recall one advertisement for an article of protection against fire. After utilizing our first three fundamentals the ad summarized with this No. 4 fundamental: "You never know when the red hazard will strike against your home and family. So act now and be sure you have taken this low-price precaution against a possible high-priced fire."

How a Salesman Uses This Factor

It is difficult to describe, in an abstract way, the many methods by which this fourth fundamental may be introduced and used. Its use usually suggests itself as the advertisement is being written. Perhaps the best way to isolate it here for definition and description might be to compare it to the procedure of a salesman as he nears the close of a sales talk.

For example, the salesman may say, "And now, Mr. Blank, I know you will realize from the statements I have already made that this product will save you a considerable amount of money, a great deal of your time, and much unnecessary work. I have given you proof of what it has done for many other people. The facts and figures I have cited prove that no expense has been spared in assuring that the quality of this product is what you would naturally expect in any product put out by a well-known firm such as ours. [No. 2 and No. 3 here, above.]

"But I would also like you to picture in your own mind why it is so desirable for you to enjoy immediately the advantages which this product offers to you. Surely the saving of one hundred dollars a year means as much to you as it does to those other people whose experiences I have mentioned.

"And, of course, saving almost one hour a day is likewise very much worthwhile to you. I know that you can think of many more interesting things you could do with this extra time in these busy days! That is why I really think it would be very much to your advantage to accept this opportunity at once. Another reason why immediate action on your part is worthwhile is that, at the present time [now going on to Fundamental No. 5, *Ask for Action*] our company is offering a special discount to those who . . ."

Of course, in a printed advertisement, your copy may not cover Fundamental No. 4 in just this way. But I believe that this close of a sales talk illustrates (and, I hope, isolates) this factor—and shows how, as compared with No. 2 factors, the No. 4 elements are more of a summary, more of a preparation for the final step of asking for some specific action.

It May Be Negative or Positive

If the main body of your advertisement is positive in nature, showing the advantages to be gained through the use of your product, then this No. 4 factor near the end of the advertisement may perhaps be negative—showing what the prospect will lose by not purchasing.

One writer refers to this element as "a bold summary at the end, a selling summary." It may represent the most dramatic benefit—the unexpected, or the most surprising thing—the best one to serve as an inducement to buy. It may reiterate your strongest selling point, your crusher. In fact, your headline or the lead of your first paragraph in the copy often provides the note for it.

In a longer piece of copy this fourth fundamental may even present a demonstration of specific advantages of the product in use, particularizing the general claims which have already been made for it. The value of demonstration as a selling tool is well known but it is especially well defined in an article by Walter Weir about the great Claude Hopkins:

> The greatest lesson that Hopkins has to teach—and he repeats it over and over again—is that demonstration is the best form of selling. In its purest form, it is known as sampling. But the most successful advertisements are almost always *verbal samplings* of the product or service to be sold. The advantages of either to the potential user are presented so concretely, so vividly, so dramatically, that he finds it practically demonstrated to him as he reads. He has a visual sample left on his mental doorstep.

I have noticed some interesting things about the actual style of much of the No. 4 clincher copy which appears in advertisements. It is often more intense in style than some of the copy which has preceded it. It seems to have a more emotional texture—just as one's own language may have more urgency and intensity when one is just about to ask for *action* on the part of another.

I have also noticed that this closing copy is often more staccato, with shorter sentences and a vigor of style which helps to produce, on the part of the reader, a tempo that will encourage action. These stylistic variations should be natural in form; care must be taken not to make them sound forced or insincere.

The Sixth Prune

This No. 4 factor in an advertisement is a very important one. It can be the plus factor that pushes over many a sale—the final straw that breaks the camel's back of reader inertia or resistance. It can be "The Sixth Prune" that builds a business. Do you remember the story written by Robert R. Updegraff bearing that title? It so well illustrates what I mean that I'll outline it briefly.

A woman who ran a boardinghouse always, when she served prunes for dessert, gave her "mealers" exactly five of them. She couldn't very well have given less than five, even though she would have liked to. But she never gave more. The five prunes became a rite with her . . . and a source of irritation to her boarders. The boardinghouse never went very well, and the tables were never filled.

Finally the management was taken over by another woman. Her first move was to serve six prunes instead of five. The difference was only one more prune per "mealer," but it served as a dramatic symbol of the new spirit that pervaded the general management of the boardinghouse. The one additional prune was appreciated, talked about, applauded. People who hadn't eaten there for years came back. Their renewed patronage permitted other welcome innovations and additions to the menu, and these held the newly regained trade. The boardinghouse began to make money, and finally became highly successful. All started by the Sixth Prune!

Likewise, the adept use of Fundamental No. 4 can often make all the difference in an advertisement. It can push over much on-the-fence hesitation and inertia. It can ask the reader to reconsider his true *need* for the product, now that he has just read the advantages of possessing it. Coming in as summarizing clincher copy, right before the bid for action, it can close the gap that often exists between the main body of the selling copy and the final close of the advertisement.

Important as it is, this element is nevertheless frequently omitted in advertisements. Yet, even though you may be pressed for space, this type of closing copy can and should be used. A few sentences may be all that are needed.

THE FIVE NECESSARY INGREDIENTS

In one of the interesting bulletins gotten out by the Mosely Selective List Service of Boston, good advertising is described as "building up a bright picture of value in the reader's mind which outshines the picture of price." The bulletin then continues: "Think of it as a chemical process. You introduce into the test tube the element of price and the element of value. Not until there is enough of the value element put in will there be a reaction which we call a sale."

Woodrow Wilson utilized this "added value" principle in his negotiations with Clemenceau. The "Tiger of France" had always been violently opposed to the League of Nations idea, and Wilson wondered how to win him over. Colonel House made this simple suggestion: Talk to Clemenceau about *the freedom of the seas;* that is the ONLY advantage clearly connected with the League which he wants. Wilson did. And Clemenceau's antagonism vanished. He became a stanch supporter of the League.

Aim at the Hardest Target

Every one of the five fundamentals which we are reviewing is necessary in this chemical process. Those people who are *easy* to sell may perhaps be sold even if some of these factors are left out. But it is wiser to plan your advertisement so that it will have a powerful impact upon those who are *hardest* to sell. For, unlike personalized selling, we cannot in printed advertising come to a "trial close" in our sales talk—in order to see if those who are easier to sell will welcome the dotted line without further persuasion. We must assume that we are talking to the hardest ones—and that the more thoroughly our copy sells both the hard and the easy, the better chance we have against the competition for the consumer's dollar—and also the less dependent we will be upon the usual completely ineffective follow-through on our advertising effort which later takes place at the sales counter itself.

Now let's get along to your last step in the writing of a successful advertisement: Fundamental No. 5, *Ask for Action*.

QUIZ ON CHAPTER 4

1. In what way is this fourth fundamental different from the second?

2. How did Charles M. Schwab use it to gain Andrew Carnegie's agreement to a merger?

3. Recall the example given of how a salesman used it.

4. Can it be used in either a positive or a negative way?

5. For what specific purpose may it be used effectively in a longer piece of copy?

6. Is the tempo of this particular copy often different?

7. In what ways?

8. How does the story of "The Sixth Prune" exemplify this No. 4 factor?

9. How can it close a gap between the main body and the final close of an advertisement?

10. How did Woodrow Wilson use it in his negotiations with Clemenceau?

THIRTEEN AGAINST THE GODS

One of my favorite books is *Twelve Against the Gods,* by William Bolitho. In a series of brilliant word portraits Bolitho sketches the lives of "twelve adventurers of history"—among them, Alexander the Great, Columbus, Charles XII of Sweden, Napoleon, and Woodrow Wilson.

The course of the true adventurer is parabolic, Bolitho tells us, not straight, so that at a certain point it leads "back to the cage" again. Setting out on his career with the abandon, although not the purposelessness, of a butterfly, the adventurer of history is condemned (when his development is ripe) to become a caterpillar. Once loaded with riches or recognition, he then turns cautious and hesitant.

To hold or gain what he wants, the adventurer finally compromises or plays everything safe. And in so doing he loses the sweep of imagination and daring which carried him aloft. The light and heat of him is slowly smothered by his concern about counting and protecting his gains, his position, his prestige. Then come the years of the Everlasting Nay response to the beckonings of Venture—and he is an adventurer no more.

Sometimes it does seem in one's daily work that the *twelve* might often be changed to *thirteen*—to include the businessman who once, earlier in his career, might have had the boldness, audacity and venturesome vision of a true adventurer.

For example, an agency's client may become one of the *thirteen* when a business tableau like this unfolds: A completely new advertising campaign is presented to him. He is glowingly enthusiastic about it. He is convinced that it is utterly new, yet sound; it is fresh, unique; no competitor has ever conceived anything like it; it will steal the market because it's basically right, though completely different from anything ever done in his field before. "Let's shoot it—after I think about it a bit overnight."

Then a few days later the reaction has set in. The sweep of the innovator has somehow been sideswiped. "Don't you think it a bit *too* unusual? What about making a few slight changes here and there? It's a bit risky; nothing like this has ever been done before in our field. Let's work over it a bit; we don't want to be too radical, you know!" The result (if any): just another campaign.

Or perhaps the agency head, or even his copy chief, may have become one of the thirteen. The scene might go something like this: The new copy man (who has purposely been hired in order to bring a fresh new approach to some of the agency's copy problems) now brings in a fresh new approach to one of the agency's copy problems. And, let us say, it is just that: fresh, new—but so *very, very* different from anything the agency has ever done for that client (or perhaps for anyone else) before.

The unlucky copy man may not realize it yet—but the thirteens are beginning to mass up solidly in front of him. Years and years of them. The instinctive, all-too-common No response has already formed behind the boss's venerable facial façade. And suddenly, in kindly and measured tones: "Not too bad as a copy *idea,* perhaps. But don't you think you've presented it in kind of a, shall I say, bizarre way? Work over it a bit, won't you, and tame it down some. I'd be leery about showing it to the client in just that form. It's a little *too* much off the beam, compared with what we've been doing for them right along."

And the copy man (slightly bewildered as to why they hired a new dog to do old tricks) wanders off, wondering just how he's going to put a much more commonplace suit of inappropriate clothes on his radically new copy idea—and still have it look any different from the type of job he was hired *not* to do!

Perhaps it would be a salutary thing if we thought of *ourselves* as ad-*venturers*—and acted like it more often in our contacts with our clients and with our own personnel.

CHAPTER 5

ASK FOR ACTION

When Cicero completed an oration, people used to say: "What a marvelous orator! What an excellent speech!"

But when Demosthenes thundered his denunciation of Philip of Macedon, people leaped to their feet. Roaring with rage, they shouted: "LET US MARCH AGAINST PHILIP!"

The same is true of advertising. One advertisement will cause readers to comment upon its being well written, attractive, and convincing. Another advertisement will not only capture attention, hold interest, and win conviction . . . but also *get action*.

As John Caples says in *Advertising for Immediate Sales*:

There are a lot of good advertisements that are weak in the final urge to act. They are like salesmen who are charming talkers but weak closing men. If they had the right stuff they would pick the reader up by the collar of his coat and the seat of his trousers and stiff-arm him into a showroom. But, instead, these advertisements leave him sitting placidly in his chair, turning the pages of a magazine or newspaper.

Open a magazine or newspaper yourself. What a tremendous number of "actionless" advertisements you see. Many of them are attractive, do a good display and copy job, and are perfect (and even prize-winning) examples of powerful and persuasive advertising—*except in this final urge*.

IF YOU REALLY WANT IT, ASK FOR IT

Now, to get action you've got to ask for it. Perhaps you remember the story about Henry Ford, Sr., talking with an old crony who suddenly asked him, "Henry, why don't you ever buy any bolts from me?" "Heck, Joe," Mr. Ford replied, "you never asked me!"

Many advertisements fail to do just that. They end without even *trying* to get the reader to translate into some sort of action the interest, the desire, and the conviction which the advertisement itself has created. All the hard-won ground already gained in the advance toward a sale is allowed to be dissipated by natural human inertia. Such advertisements *do nothing whatever* to convince the reader that this is a better time than any other to take some action about actually getting what he has just been made to want.

If a salesman neglects to make a good close he can make another call. But a "poor-closing" or a "nonclosing" advertisement makes an ineffective visit to every one of its prospects. It neglects, on every single visit that it makes, to go the full possible distance toward getting the business.

The Gap Between Reading and Acting

Perhaps one clue to the reason so much advertising produces so little action is given in this remark by Kenneth Goode and Carroll Rheinstrom in *More Profits from Advertising:*

"But," the young copy writer will protest, "if I have shown people my goods through crystal-clear copy, and drawn their desires as a magnet a needle, haven't I done a pretty handsome job? Won't the poor fish do something for themselves?"

The answers are, respectively: (1) You have. (2) They won't. Pouring water on a duck's back out of an eye dropper makes as lasting an impression on it as an ordinary advertisement makes on the average man—unless, either the advertisement or the man himself crystallizes it into terms of beneficial action. The gap between reading words and doing things is wide and wasteful.

What Kind of Action Shall We Ask For?

What steppingstones can we use to lessen this gap between the advertising in the publications and the consumer at the counter, so that the jump to a sale will be quicker, easier, and more certain?

We have said that we are going to be sure to ask for action. What kind of action are we going to ask for? Of course, it depends on the product or proposition you are selling, but I think we may divide the forms of "asking for action" into three principal categories.

THE FIRST FORM

The first form is the very common "Go to Your Dealer" type. This is usually used on impulse items, products of food, drink, and other inexpensive products in everyday use; but it is also often the complete, the only, and the final "close" depended upon to put over the sale of an expensive product.

This very meager bid for action is often tacked on at the end without any tie-up with the rest of the copy. It can be strengthened by a closer tie-up with the reasons given in the copy as to why the reader should go to his dealer—what advantages he will gain if he does so quickly, and what ones he will lose if he delays.

In other words, this simplest form of asking for action is better than none at all; but it usually seems stuck on the end as an afterthought and not as an integrated part of the advertisement. It is at least one little steppingstone across the gap between the advertisement and the sales counter; yet, as it is generally used, it is a pretty ineffective and wobbly one.

THE SECOND FORM

The second form does not necessarily ask the reader that an inquiry be made direct to the advertiser nor does it offer him anything for an inquiry at the dealer's. But it does suggest to the reader something to *do* which will establish a closer bond between himself and the advertiser or his product. It gives the reader some interesting action to carry out which will make him more friendly to the advertiser's product.

David E. Rowan calls this type of advertising "Do-Something" copy. In describing it, he mentions that it

(1) Provides the prospect with the basis for immediate action in the general direction of making a purchase, instead of leaving him hanging in mid-air with nothing much to do about the message he has been exposed to. (2) It heightens interest. Not everybody will take the time to carry through the suggested performance, but many people like to play around with an interesting experiment or demonstration. (3) It increases conviction by making it possible for the prospect to work out a sales point in terms of his own specific experience. (4) It insures a more lasting memory value for the product and the message.

Some examples of this "Do-Something" type of copy are:

A telephone company printed a list of ten important ways of using their service, asking the executive to check those ways he had used, with the suggestion that in doing so he might come across some ideas he'd like to know more about.

A brake-lining company featured diagrams of four driving situations, asking the reader to determine which car, in each diagram, was in the wrong.

A vacuum-cleaner company used, in an advertisement, a joint questionnaire for husband and wife—listing the eleven features of its product and asking the husband and wife to check at home which features seemed most important to each of them. Thus the way was paved for a joint home conference about the purposes and advantages of a vacuum cleaner.

This second form can be used alone—or it can be used in conjunction with either of the other two factors of action we are talking about here. Even if this type of copy does not close with a more direct bid for action, it nevertheless may serve a purpose by inducing the reader to do something which has an association with the product advertised. Thus it helps to impress the reader more fully with the benefits and advantages which this product offers him.

THE THIRD FORM

The third common form of "asking for action" copy is that pulling for a direct response from readers: for inquiries for a free booklet, a sample of the product, a recipe book, a free trial offer, for an entry in a contest, for a miniature model, or some gadget, novelty, or game tying up in some way with the product itself. (In a later chapter, No. 7, we will discuss various ways to increase—or decrease—the flow of inquiries.)

Besides its use as a copy-testing device, pulling for a direct response of some kind gives you a means of selling your prospect more thoroughly upon your product, or provides leads if you sell through salesmen.

Here are some of the specific ways to press for immediate action:

Make an Offer. Use a "hook"—offer a booklet, liberal sample, free demonstration or trial, an extra premium, some novelty which is relevantly tied up with the use of your product, introductory price, miniature model, contest, combination inducement, chart, free fitting, alterations or installation; entry in a contest, swatches, special phone rates for ordering, or other motivating inducement.

Time Limit. Give a time limit on your offer if you can and if such an offer is bona fide.

Limited Supply. If available supply of product is limited, or if quick action for better selection is necessary, point this fact out forcefully.

Price Going Up. If price of product is going up, emphasize that fact—giving specific date if possible. (The threat of loss unless the reader acts quickly.)

Price Down. If price of product has been reduced, use that fact to emphasize desirability of taking advantage of it at once.

Gain or Loss. Stress again what your reader gains by purchasing product immediately—or what he loses daily by not owning it.

Guarantee. If product is guaranteed, stress that this assurance removes cause for delay or inaction.

Guarantees Get Action

Because they help to induce immediate action on the part of prospects who are hesitant (and how many aren't?), guarantees have probably been offered by sellers ever since the members of the human race started to trade with each other. To get fairly recent about it, historically speaking, an advertisement which appeared in 1773 reads: "Excellent good Bohea Tea, imported in the last ship from London; sold by Theo. Hancock, *N.B.* If it don't [*sic*] suit the ladies' taste, they may return the tea and receive their money again."

Yet, despite its age-old proven effectiveness, we still see innumerable advertisements where no guarantee of any kind is offered. (In one recent issue of a national magazine only one of ninety advertisers backed up his claims with a money-back guarantee!) And, where this deliberate neglect or simple oversight is even more serious, many of these advertisements are trying to sell new products in competition with solidly entrenched brands, or expensive products, or ones where the quality of the product is so outstanding that a guarantee of dramatic and almost irresistible liberality could be extended with complete safety.

In fact, except in cases where the quality of the product is shoddy or it performs its function poorly (or where the copy about it has grossly exaggerated or misrepresented its value), experienced advertisers know that only a tiny percentage of their customers will take advantage of the refund privilege . . . and that this percentage is infinitesimal compared with the increased business which a good guarantee can stimulate.

What kind of guarantee? As liberal as you can possibly make it. "Give until it hurts"—*and until you have positive bookkeeping proof that it does hurt.* Full, or double, money-back; partial money-back; with a time limit, or even without one; with a refund of transportation costs in addition; with a reason on the part of the purchaser, or without one, "no questions asked"; guarantee of free repairs or free replacement, or function as promised, of every claim made in the advertising, or each single ingredient *in* the product; upon return of the unused portion of the product, or not; the particularly effective free trial or free examination, without payment in advance.

One form of guarantee which has proven to be a salutary sales stimulant is based upon proof of performance. An interesting example of it (in *double* guarantee form) was made in connection with the sale of a book of golf instruction. The first, and more commonly used, part of the guarantee assured the purchaser that his money would be refunded if his examination of the book did not convince him that it would improve his game. The second and proof-of-performance part of it assured him of a full refund if, by putting into actual practice the instruction given in the book, he did not (within a specified length of time) cut a specific number of strokes from his score.

The advertisements carried a panel containing two columns of figures. The column at the left was headed "If Your Score Now Averages"; the one at the right, "It Will Come Down This Much—If You Do What This Book Tells You." At the bottom of the panel, across both columns, it said, "Or Your Money Will Be Cheerfully Refunded in Full."

There are many different types of guarantee. However, whatever one is made should be stated so clearly and simply that the extent of its coverage is beyond misinterpretation. You should also be sure to check it first with the rulings which have been set forth by the Federal Trade Commission.

MAKE IT SIMPLE—EASY—SPECIFIC

Now, no matter what form of action you ask your reader to take, make this action as simple and easy and specific as you can.

Ask yourself: "What do I want people to *do* when they finish reading my copy? How, where, and when do I want them to do it?" For example, here is a little list of some of the information which John Caples found in various advertisements, facts which made it easier for people to act immediately:

- the exact location—"600 Fifth Avenue, *at 48th St.*"

- the phone number, and what department or individual to call

- the number of the floor—"Suits, Third Floor"

- how to get to the advertiser's location—"D Train, Independent Subway, E. Broadway Station"

- a drawing of an auto map, with an X marking the location

- a phrase telling the delivery charge for areas beyond free-delivery sections

- instructions on "how to measure" when ordering textiles

- exactly "what to say" when ordering certain items by phone

- full details about easy-payment plans, to facilitate an immediate favorable decision

- mail-order coupons to use "if you cannot shop at our store for this sale *tomorrow*"

- the hours, and evenings, when the shop is open

If you are giving people a choice of style, color, model, or design, make that choice as simple as possible. You know what happens when a clerk spreads too many neckties out on the counter. The prospect gets bewildered, decides he will have to think it over, buys nothing.

"Delay Is the Enemy of a Sale"

It is said that "delay is the enemy of a sale." The word "murderer" could almost replace "enemy." Retail stores know that when adverse weather interferes with shopping, a considerable part of the purchases are not merely postponed: they are lost forever.

So remove any obstacles which stand in front of action on the part of the prospect—those which make it harder or less convenient for him to respond at once, or those which confuse him, make him indecisive, and lead to no action at all. For, as George B. Hotchkiss tells us: "Human beings have a tremendous amount of inertia. Consequently the advertiser often finds it wise to end his appeal with positive stimulants to action. The most common methods are the following: (1) By direct command; (2) by removing obstacles and inhibitions; (3) by offering inducements; (4) by making action easy."

As Richard Manville once said: "Don't think about advertisements —think about people." Therefore, think how you personally induce someone to take an action when you are in conversation with him. You make it worth his while and you make it easy for him to do so. That is the way to think of it when you are working out this fifth fundamental of an advertisement.

The Fallacy of "Sometime"

We have just talked about making it easy—and making it worth-while—for your reader to take some action after reading your advertisement. Now let us give an example of what we mean by pressing for *immediate* action. Has this ever happened to you? Your friends have had a nice evening at your home. Yet their "good-by" (clipped a bit) runs like this: "We've had such a lovely time. You simply must visit us. We'll look forward to it."

No "hook." No definite date, such as: "And now we want you to visit US! How is next Tuesday night—at 8:30?"

Try to make a "definite date" with the readers of your advertising. Don't let them trail off. If you possibly can, give them something specific to do *at once*. "Always give others a choice between *something and something*," says Elmer Wheeler, "not between *something* and *nothing*." So try to get people to take action of some kind which will lead them nearer to the sales counter itself. An advertisement which virtually closes with "Why don't you come up and see me SOMETIME?" is a long way from a sale.

"BOX OFFICE" TELLS THE STORY

The purpose of most advertising is simple: to make people buy— a product, a service, or an idea. Not just to make them pause, or admire, or even merely to believe. Advertising is nothing but an expense —not an investment—unless it gets action: the kind of action that will pay a profit.

Therefore, the ultimate value of advertising is determined by the quantity and quality of the sales action it produces. And your own ability in the use of this fifth fundamental of a good advertisement (*Ask for Action*) can determine the final effectiveness of everything else you have put into it.

Of course, ratings on tests of opinion, memory value, recognition, unaided recall, or other check-up methods may give the copy man significant information. But, as Walter Weir puts it, "The best copy testing machine is still a cash register." In the final analysis, this is the biggest point of all: Is the advertising producing action on the part of its readers?

When Gatti-Casazza, the famous opera impresario, asked the composer Verdi for advice regarding the duties of an impresario, Verdi told him: "Read most attentively the reports of the box office. These, whether you like it or not, are the only documents which measure success or failure and they admit of no argument and represent not mere opinion but fact. If the public comes, the object is attained; if not—no! The theater is intended to be full and not empty. That's something you must always remember."

Not What People Say—but What They Do

Similarly, if your ad doesn't get action on the part of the public, it doesn't matter what rating it wins in any consumer-reaction test that is divorced from sales figures themselves and doesn't take into account actual box-office pull.

After the campaign appears, it is then too late for the post mortems: what Jim Woolf calls the "doctors of hindsight" say about it. And what about the *prejudging* of advertisements—by "typical consumers" asked to give their opinion as to relative effectiveness? Are their opinions (*unless supported by dependable evidence*) worth gambling any advertising expenditure upon? Having suddenly been elevated from the position of potential purchasers whose money is actually involved in their choice of products and the persuasiveness of advertising appeals into the professional status of expert "judges" and thus also "critics" of advertisements—they have put on an entirely different uniform. What their unsupported opinions are worth can be gathered from Somerset Maugham's passage about dramatic critics:

> But the critic is there not to feel but to judge. He must hold aloof from the contagion that has captured the group and keep his self-possession. He must not allow his heart to carry him away; his head must remain well screwed on his shoulders. He must take care not to become part of the audience. He is not there to play his part in the play, but to watch it from the outside. The result is that he does not see the play they see because he has not, as they have, acted in it.

The Battle for the Bucks

In the first chapter of this book you have read about the battle each advertisement must put up in order to get attention. It is appropriate to conclude this present chapter by pointing out why the "Battle for the Bucks" makes this *Ask for Action* part of your advertisement so vitally important.

Some years ago I made a survey of the advertising content of a certain national magazine. The magazine contained 450 advertisements. The total retail price of the products advertised in it was $8,559.19. Surveys made by the advertising manager of the magazine indicated that the average annual income of his readers was about $3,808.00 per family. Thus, in *one* monthly issue, these 450 advertisers were asking the reader to spend more than 2¼ times what he made in a full year!

This fierce competition for the consumer's dollar is of course not merely confined to products of the same nature as yours. Your advertising is also actually fighting for consumer action against products not *in themselves* competitive with your own. The conflict is general, ruthless, constant, unending. Luxuries contend against necessities. Recently developed products fight for their new lives. Long-established ones slug it out with "interlopers."

Obviously, in this ferocious "battle for the bucks," advertising which asks for action so effectively that it gets it not only gives its direct competitors a mighty hard time, but also gets a part of the consumer's dollar which would otherwise be spent upon some completely noncompetitive product or service.

QUIZ ON CHAPTER 5

1. Pick up any magazine. Count the number of advertisements which do not *ask for action* in any form whatever, even the simplest.

2. Describe the first form of asking for action.

3. Describe the second form.

4. Describe the third form.

5. Name seven ways to press for immediate action.

6. Should you offer a guarantee, if you possibly can?

7. How liberal should you make it?

8. What is meant by the fallacy of "sometime"?

9. What is "the best copy-testing machine"?

10. Why does the competitive situation make good *ask for action* copy so necessary?

THE UNBEATABLE BRIEF CASE

For a number of years I have watched copy men come and go—and come up and go down. And I've come to this pretty fixed conclusion: that a copy man with brief case attached makes a hard combination to beat.

Brilliance itself is a nice thing to have . . . if you can keep living up to it. Inspiration alone is a grand kind of lightning to be struck by . . . if you can make it strike like a trip hammer. But I've noticed that the

Brief Case Boy is usually the tireless tortoise who eventually takes the race away from the dazzling hare.

And by a Brief Case Boy I mean exactly this: a copy man who really *likes* a brief case. He loves to cram it full of stuff and, without resentment or self-pity, to lug it home with him. The stuff may be assignments that weren't even scheduled to be finished today, or they may be unassigned ideas of his own that he wants to slap on the chief's desk tomorrow. In either case, he is eager to "get at 'em," do them well, and get on to the next job.

This isn't an Alger story, even though it may sound like one. It's a fact. Reasonably good daily work, "during hours," can usually (although not even *always*) hold the job down and, if done well, win periodic raises. But the "brief case time," after hours, is the *plus* factor that can give the big push to a copy man. *This* is the time which, away from the interruptions and the routine, can do the real paying off.

For the funny thing about it is that just plain garden-variety plugging does have a way of blooming into copywriting brilliance. After a while, perspiration exudes inspiration. Ask the shades of prolific, indefatigable men like Balzac, Tolstoi, Wagner, da Vinci, Zola, Browning, Voltaire, Raphael!

No matter *how* inexpert a copy man you may think you now are, you just can't keep filling a brief case with extra hours and not pull a bigger job out of it. For what else can the boss do about it? If he's a boss worth working for at all, what else *can* he do with a man who keeps pouring it on—using time he isn't paid for to present the firm with new ideas and copy—work that gets better and better as his extra hours and effort begin inevitably to prove that "the more doing, the better done"?

No little talk of this kind is complete unless Napoleon is brought into it. So here he comes. Certain officers of his staff came to him one day to urge the promotion of one of his captains.

"Why do you suggest *this* man?" asked the general. The officers then explained that the captain, by his brilliant strategy, had won an important battle a few days before.

"Good," said Napoleon, "but what did he do the *next* day?"

If you do not feel that, as yet, you are too hot as a copy man, some commuting with that little brown or black bag can make you good. If you are now a good copy man it can make you better. And if you are one of those whose copy and ideas are, like Napoleon's captain, occasionally brilliant, it can even step up your batting average.

My personal nomination for a heraldic shield for the advertising business would be an obese brief case, rampant on a field of copy paper.

———————

CHAPTER 6

HOW LONG SHOULD THE COPY BE?

Can all the five fundamentals we have discussed be present in each ad? Won't that make the copy too long? We shall soon try to answer the question as to what is "too long." But first let me say that the fundamentals of a good advertisement can be worked into even a very short piece of copy. To carry this to the very extreme of conciseness, you can show people an advantage in one sentence. (In that case, it would of course be your major and most persuasive one.) You can prove it in one sentence, using your most powerful piece of evidence. In another single sentence you can urge people to grasp this advantage. And in your final sentence you can clearly specify the action you want your reader to take.

Yes, it can be done. But how well can it be done? That question leads us to another, one which because of its importance is discussed more frequently (usually with more heat than light) than almost any other phase of copywriting: How long should the copy be?

Platitudes Won't Answer This Question

The perennial question of "copy length" admits of no simple, pat answer. Actually, as you will see from the following analysis, it broadens out into *all the* phases of the writing of an advertisement which we have already discussed. Platitudes and generalities on so specific a question can be used only to excuse or to rationalize a course of action. Copy is, in effect, an application for a particular job—and should be long enough to do the job you have set for it.

104

Therefore step-by-step analysis is first necessary. And, later, analysis on your own part will help to guide you toward an intelligent decision on each particular job confronting you.

One answer often given to the question which heads this chapter merely repeats Lincoln's reply to the man who inquired how long a man's leg should be: "Long enough to reach the ground."

That answer doesn't get copy men very far. Now if someone asked how long a man's *arms* should be, and if Lincoln had replied, "Long enough to grasp whatever object he wants to reach"—then the story might give copy men a clue. For an advertisement does, in effect, reach its arms out of a publication toward an objective: some degree of response, either in thought or action.

Therefore, first decide your objective. How far along the road to a completed sale do you want that particular advertisement to propel your reader?

Eight Milestones to a Sale

Review in your mind the milestones that stud this road. Let us list them in the order of a reader's reactions to a successful advertisement:

1. This advertisement got my attention.
2. Its headline won my interest.
3. This interest carried me into the first paragraph.
4. The first paragraph got me to go on reading the copy.
5. This copy held my interest, convinced me; so . . .
6. That product must be good; and . . .
7. I will get it *sometime,* or . . .
8. I am going to get it *NOW*.

Which milestone do you want to reach? For a retailed product you will want to come as near the No. 8 goal as possible. If you happen to be writing a mail-order advertisement your objective is to accomplish that No. 8 objective. If it does not do so it is not a good mail-order advertisement.

How much does copy length have to do with reaching your objective? Before I go into that question I want to point out that if you compare advertisements of commercial products of today with those of even a relatively few years ago you will discover a pronounced trend toward longer copy.

The guidance given in this chapter does not seek to justify long copy on everything, but it analyzes the validity of the still all-too-common fear of longer copy on anything. And it also attempts to help you decide when to use longer or shorter copy—dependent upon circumstances. So first let us see what bearing copy length has upon this eight-milestone job of the *conversion* of reader attention into reader action.

The Qualities of Quantity

We shall first consider quantity of copy only, regardless of its quality. We are doing this for five reasons:

1. Criticism of an unsuccessful advertisement is based generally on headline, layout, art work, theme, quality of copy, media used—but almost never on having *too little* copy.

2. Advertisers with prejudices against copy they arbitrarily say is "too long" are inclined, themselves, to judge it quantitatively only.

3. It simplifies our discussion at this point. Because quantity is absolute, quality is not. One hundred words are one hundred words, whether they are good copy or poor.

4. Advertisers who sell through retailers must find the "quantitative" answer to "how long should the copy be?"—if they want their advertisements to come as near as possible to the before-mentioned No. 8 goal: converting more readers into customers, sending more of them to dealers as fully presold as copy can make them.

5. Advertisers who are able to check their advertising and sales results carefully have discovered an astonishing relationship between effectiveness and number of words used. They have found that—unless copy is exceptionally fine or exceptionally bad—these ratios of resultfulness to copy length are fairly constant.

You can apply to advertising copy Socrates' remark that "Whether the instances you select be men or dogs, or anything else, few are the extremes, but many are in the mean between them." Likewise, all copy is more likely to be either fair or good than either bad or fine. A superlative and inspired piece of copy may (like great people or works of genius in any field of endeavor) break all the rules and still accomplish its purpose. It may omit one or more of the five fundamentals we have discussed. Likewise, it may bring the desired results —even though it may not be as long as copy in other successful advertisements on the same proposition. But production of such exceptional copy does not occur often enough for any advertiser to risk limiting the length of *all* copy solely to "make it shorter."

YOU ARE AN EVANGELIST

We have used the word "conversion" to describe turning reader attention into reader action. It's an accurate word for this transition; and it will carry our reasoning along, relevantly, if we compare two examples of conversion: the effort of copy to convert a reader into a customer—and (without irreverence, but merely for clarity and verisimilitude) the effort of an evangelist on a public platform trying to win converts. The two efforts are comparable in these ways:

1. Your copy is, in purpose, "commercially evangelistic." You are trying to make people "hit the sawdust trail" toward your product.

2. Both advertisement and platform speaker must first get attention, or neither will be addressing anyone.

3. Both convey a message to an audience of human beings varied in backgrounds, intelligence, circumstances, and innumerable other respects.

4. Some in both audiences are fairly easy to convince; some, very hard; others, between these two extremes. Some are quicker to act than others.

5. Some in both audiences have ingrown prejudices, or established habits, which run counter to the appeal being made.

6. To some, in both audiences, the message is of great immediate interest; the interest of others, at the start, may be as casual as that of an onlooker whose attention has been caught or his curiosity aroused.

7. Similarly, any in *your* audience, too, can walk out any time.

That establishes enough factors of logical comparison. So let us carry this analogy a step further.

What does the evangelist do to make as many converts as possible? Does his experience indicate that a talk running the risk of being too short (even though intrinsically good) can safely be depended upon to produce the full degree of listener action he wants?

No, he keeps his audience with him as *long* as he can. That is the only way to make sufficient progress with the varied audience which he (and your advertisement) faces. Based on the law of averages, the longer he can hold interest, the more people will he convince—and the greater will be the number who will inevitably walk forward and "hit the sawdust trail." The less able he is to hold interest for a sufficient time, the greater will be the number who will inevitably walk out.

Yet the evangelist has one advantage. He can see how many are walking out; and he can use new elements of persuasion if the exodus looks too great. The advertisement you are writing cannot.

A LOGICAL OBSERVATION

Where does this analogy get us? *Regardless of how long or short your copy may be,* the analogy leads to this observation:

The LONGER your copy can hold the interest of the greatest number of readers, the likelier you are to induce MORE of them to act.

And now (as with the evangelist's audience) the law of averages plays a big part in what happens. For you must first realize fully the many implications of the fact that, although your advertisement is printed by the thousands, people read it one by one.

What you, as one individual, have irrevocably written must now meet the test of interest and appeal to thousands of individuals, each a heterogeneous mixture. The response, both in degree and total, will depend upon its interest to each reader as an individual.

Relatively few among those thousands will be "very easy" to sell: "in the market" for your product at that time; not primarily concerned with price; not "wedded to" a competitive product; quick to act. A greater number will be "very hard" to sell: only casually interested at that time; with price or "bargain value" a major consideration; competition-minded; slow to act.

How Far Will You Carry the Majority?

The vast majority of your readers will be between those two extremes. For the above, or a myriad of other reasons, they will be easier or harder to sell than others. And this vast majority, in addition to those in the "very hard to sell" group, will at best (unless you can hold interest *longer*) merely reach the previously mentioned No. 6 goal: agreeing that the product is good, but not moved to act. Because the sludge of human inertia is so stagnant that too small an amount of copy cannot make that sludge flow into action—unless (and usually even though) the *quality* of the copy, or the inherent appeal of the product, is tremendously far above average. And it's a rare copy idea that can be presented with great brevity and still get immediate action.

To sum up: The *longer* your copy can hold people the more of them you will sell; and the more interesting your copy *is,* the longer you will hold them. If you can keep your reader interested, you will have a better chance of propelling him to action. If you cannot do that, then too small an amount of copy won't push him far enough along that road anyway.

The Vital Key Word

Therefore, "interest" is our key word—bringing us to these three points:

1. What subject interests readers most?

2. How can you write about that subject so that you hold him longer, in spite of the number of words necessary to get the degree of response you want?

3. How can you make this longer copy more inviting, physically— less formidable in appearance?

We'll tackle No. 1—What subject interests your reader most? Himself, and his family. So, as explained more fully in earlier chapters, your copy subject is what your product will do for him, or for his family.

It's amazing how much copy any person will read, willingly, if it continues to point out these consumer benefits; if you keep making your product win advantages for him.

Continuously interesting presentation of strong consumer-benefit sales angles justifies and rewards the use of longer copy. That does not mean just adding words. Apropos is the story of the old man suing his wife for divorce. The judge asked what grounds he had. "Judge," he answered, "she just talk and talk—all day." The judge inquired, "What does she talk about?" The reply was, "She don't say."

The Quantity of Quality

Now we leave this quantitative part of the story and come to our *qualitative* second point: how to make your copy hold interest in your subject longer.

Unreadable copy goes unread. Readability makes longer copy seem shorter. The copy man's or the advertiser's conception of readability is not necessarily the reader's. What isn't worth reading from the standpoint of the prospect isn't worth telling in expensive advertising space. A great deal of advertising has no vital interest, except to the man who pays or it; and if he were not paying for it, even *he* would not trouble to read the copy, short or long.

Therefore, since holding interest longer with readable copy has so much bearing on final cash-register results, we are now going to review ways to do it. Let's itemize some of those ideas which (because of their specific effectiveness in sustaining interest) deserve listing.

22 Ways to Hold Interest Longer

1. Start copy with a pertinent question, to help get people into it. Commence certain paragraphs with such questions. Throughout the

copy, work in questions that stimulate interest in answers to follow. They also provide an interesting change of pace and style.

2. Or begin with your strongest consumer-benefit fact.

3. Give copy news value. Put news (and most newsworthy item of it) into first paragraph. What is stale news to the advertiser may be fresh news to the reader—and vice versa.

4. Avoid vague generalities. Be concrete, specific. Tell who, what, when, where, why, how.

5. Speedily identify copy with needs and desires of reader.

6. Stick to buying points, concerning reader, not selling points, concerning advertiser. Sell people advantages, not things.

7. Select sales angles with greatest general appeal. Concentrate on them. Don't clutter up copy with minor claims.

8. Get in plenty of emotional appeal. Long novels often become best sellers, but even short books of logic rarely do.

9. Touch people on points of common human contact. Make them say, "Yes, that is just like me."

10. Avoid flat claims. Use vivid portrayal of dramatic situations, humanized facts, word pictures to inspire reader to want, as soon as possible, what the product will do for, and get for, him.

11. Put as much personality, human interest, showmanship into it as you can, with naturalness.

12. Try to make it entertaining to read. More adults go to movies than to schools of instruction.

13. Make copy relevant to product, not filled with distractive influences.

14. Use subheads having news (or relevant curiosity) appeal—to get readers into following body matter. Consider using subheads in question form, for same reason. Or make them tell a quick, sequential sales story of their own—for the glancer.

15. Use vigorous, nonstatic style to help copy suggest action and march toward _action. Punctuate adequately, carefully, for clarity, simplicity, longer stay-with-it interest, greater urgency. (Punctuation can be made *actively* effective, not merely marks casually sprinkled out of the saltcellar of language.)

16. Use short, simple sentence construction, crystal-clear in meaning. Rebuild sentences that contain wordy circumlocutions. This isn't

easy. As Robert Louis Stevenson puts it, "It takes hard writing to make easy reading."

17. Use vivid present tense, singular instead of plural. Make it already happen to him as he reads. Jim Young once said, "To get a man to do a thing, let him see himself doing it." For example, from an airline advertisement: "You left the East Coast at one o'clock after an excellent lunch. Now, stretched out in a big, cushioned easy chair, you watch cloud patterns shift on the green and gold checkerboard of the farmland below."

18. Use active verbs, pictorial nouns.

19. Avoid too many adjectives, adverbs, pronouns, demonstrative articles, dependent clauses and phrases, subjunctive mood. Mark Twain's advice about adjectives is worth following: "As to the Adjective: when in doubt, strike it out."

20. Use vocabulary of least erudite of your prospects, then everyone will follow you. Said Ernest Hemingway, "I use the oldest words in the English language. People think I'm an ignorant bastard who doesn't know the ten-dollar words. I know the ten-dollar words. There are older and better words which if you arrange them in the proper combination you make it stick."

John Caples suggests a sound way to look at it when he says, "Don't make ads simple because you think people are low in intelligence. Some are smart and some are not smart. The point is that people are thinking about other things when they see your ad. Your ad does not get their full attention or intelligence. Your ad gets only a fraction of their intelligence. . . . People won't study your ad carefully. They can't be bothered. And so you have to make your ads simple."

Yet avoid the suggestion of condescension and "writing down" to people. It is astonishing how well people can understand any topic that really wins their interest. For example, the inside of a radio is a very complicated thing. Yet thousands learned how to build their own—simply because they were fascinated by the idea. Also, when you think of it, the operation of an automobile is in actuality not so very simple a thing to learn. Yet people who are otherwise not too bright do it and do it well—because driving gives them pleasure. It is equally astonishing to realize the number of words of which ordinary people know the meaning when these words portray advantages to them!

21. Grammatically, lead carefully from one point of interest to the next; link them clearly.

22. Finally: longer copy does not mean looser copy, mere verbiage. Keep it compact, well integrated. Its job is not to fill up white space, not to make the reader say, like Shakespeare's King John, "I was never so be-thumped with words." Its job is to propel people (through holding their interest longer) to the point of purchase—or as near to it as possible.

How to Make It Look *More Inviting*

Let us say that you have decided longer copy will better accomplish the job you have set for your advertisement. So we arrive at our third point: how to make this longer copy look more inviting physically, less formidable in appearance. You work against your own purpose if you don't make it look as inviting as its length and the amount of your space permit. These are just a few ideas on how it may be done.

1. Paragraphs—Short. Indented, not flush. Double lead between each. Occasionally centered. Judicious use of italics, caps, bold face, or oversize initials.

2. Copy blocks—Not too wide for proper eye range in relation to type size. Vary widths. Graduation of type size; setting the opening paragraphs in a larger size, then dropping to smaller.

3. Subheads—Frequent and bold enough to break up any too formidable appearance of body matter; but not enough to distract reader from sequential flow of copy story.

Consider use of a two-or-three-sentence introductory-display subhead between headline and opening body matter—to get reader into latter.

4. Type size—As large as is consistent with copy length you have decided will best accomplish your ultimate purpose. Remember that, if you hold interest, people will read much smaller type (thus en-

abling you to use more of your most telling sales angles) than you may have ever imagined.

5. White space—As much as is consistent with objective mentioned above. Although some amount of white space will help you get attention, every unnecessary line of it deletes copy which is more likely to gain your objective than will the white space it has replaced.

6. Art work—Not for mere decoration, but to advance, or substantiate, copy story pictorially. Remember that the amount of space which it occupies *unnecessarily and without furtherance of that purpose* eats up space for selling copy that would be more resultful.

7. Specification matter—Product specifications, or similar technical details, may sometimes be set in smaller type, boxed. They are there for those who want to know them; but they do not interfere with more attractive display of the more highly motivated copy.

The Form vs. *Substance Mistake*

Your object in using these and other devices is to make body matter look more inviting—but without allowing these devices to interfere with, or detract from, the well-thought-out sequence of your copy story. Two things to remember concerning that fact:

1. Remember this statement by G. Lynn Sumner: "Do not lose faith in the eternal effectiveness of advertising copy. Remember that users of 'fashion' in advertising technique are primarily working for attention. Nothing can take the place of *copy* for persuasion, for downright selling. Fashions in advertising may come and go, but they never lessen the power of the printed word."
So avoid the common copywriting error of relying on form instead of on substance—but make that selling substance as interesting, both in content and appearance, as you can.

2. Physically irrelevant devices detract from the interest in, and readability of, that substance.

A Condensed Recapitulation

Now, before going into the second section of this discussion, let's take time out for a condensed recapitulation.

1. Decide how far along the road to immediate action you want to make your advertisement propel your reader.

2. Copy length has a bearing on how well your advertisement accomplishes this purpose.

3. Because, the longer you can make your copy hold the interest of the greatest number of your readers, the more likely it is to do whatever you want it to do.

4. Therefore—since people are more interested in themselves and families than in anything else—your general subject will be, What this product will do for my reader.

5. But, specifically, there are certain more readable and more interesting ways to tell this copy story of consumer benefits. These will hold the interest of more readers longer and better than other ways. So—to propel people (through holding interest) to the point of purchase, or as near to it as possible—consider the twenty-two ways reviewed previously.

6. Also, there are certain ways to make the body matter of copy look more inviting physically—without interfering with the flow of the copy story.

HOW TO DECIDE THE BEST COPY LENGTH

Now we're going to consider how to decide and adjust your copy length in accordance with the limitations and circumstances you face on a specific job. But before we do that we must make some general observations—and a few concerning certain fetishes and misconceptions.

First, many advertisers do not realize the tremendous potential power of copy. They don't demand enough from it, don't make it work hard enough. They say, "Well, that's as far as copy can go." Yet that is often the point where it is just beginning to sell.

Put more of the selling burden upon the shoulders of your copy, even though it may make it longer. Delay is the enemy of sale. A postponed sale may be lost forever. The more fully your copy sells the reader, the nearer and quicker it will get him to the sales counter —and (when it gets him there) the less you will rely upon notoriously incapable "salesmanship" at the counter, or worry about brand switching.

Not that it is wise or necessary for all advertisers to follow the mail-order man's maxim: "Tell people you are going to tell them, then tell them, then tell them you've told them." A mail-order advertisement's job is extra tough; that is why some highly successful examples contain 1,500 to 2,000 words, or even more.

Yet remember that, strictly speaking, NON-mail-order copy has the same necessity for reader motivation; actually, the principles peculiar to mail-order advertising are those connected, directly or indirectly, with the effort to induce the reader to *write* to the advertiser and to do so at once.

It's Easier to Get Attention and Interest than to Hold It

Copywriters have, through various devices, attained more skill in getting attention and interest than in holding it. This may consciously or subconsciously stem from the influence of the maxim, "It is harder to write short copy than long," or Madame de Sévigné's remark, "Had I more time I would have written you a shorter letter." Or as Lincoln said about an indolent lawyer who wrote an overlong "brief": "Reminds me of the lazy preacher who used to write long sermons. His explanation was that he got to writing and was too lazy to stop."

These statements are sometimes true of copywriters who are neither energetic nor resourceful enough to write good copy of a greater length than they are accustomed to handle, nor capable enough to write superlatively effective shorter copy. (In other words, if a copywriter is incapable of making it interesting, he'd *better* make it short!)

However, any copy on any product can be made interesting. It is up to the copy writer. As Gilbert K. Chesterton said: "There is no such thing on earth as an uninteresting subject; the only thing that can exist is an uninterested person."

The Everlasting Yea and Nay

We have already discussed many reasons for longer copy. But worth emphasis here is that it can combine both positive and negative appeals.

By taking enough length to use both positive and negative sales angles, you influence a larger number of minds and people. "Is it not a mistaken idea," writes F. B. McLeary, "that the only way to attain force is through brevity? Fights sometimes end in the first round with a single knockout blow, but more often the defeated boxer takes the count as a result of a rain of lighter punches directed to vulnerable parts of the head and body."

Another reason worth repeating: If you want to get action from a varied audience you must stimulate emotion and substantiate with facts. To do both your copy must often necessarily be longer.

A salesman does not say, "How do you do?" speak a few words about his product, then ask you to sign the order. No; he uses enough words to get your emotions and reasoning power flowing toward a sale. If he sees his talk clicking strongly with you, he can then try a "quick close"; but, as mentioned before, your advertisement cannot.

So, if you are a logical prospect and he fails to sell you, it is because he has not told you interestingly, convincingly, and completely enough why what his product will do for you is more important to you than its price. If he succeeds, it is because his sales angles have held your interest, through the right "spoken" copy—and enough of it. Yet many advertisements virtually say little more than "Hello—Our product is wonderful—Good-by."

If It Isn't There It Can't Do Any Work

Likewise, it is obvious (but often overlooked) that no reader can be influenced by good sales angles which don't appear in the advertisement at all. Consequently, even "grasshopper readers" (who will not read the copy consecutively but simply hop around in it and sample what interests them most) can't be sold enough unless they are told enough.

In other words, if these sales angles aren't in the copy, then even your grasshopper readers can't be influenced by them. But if they are there, they at least have a chance of influencing *all* your readers. And you cannot shorten copy too much, merely for the greater attraction of some people, without running the risk of leaving too little of it to do a good job of selling the others.

Attempting to compromise with this fact, many advertisers try, in effect, to make a deal with the reader. They make dull advertisements short. Yet mere brevity does not make an otherwise dull advertisement interesting—any more than mere length makes an otherwise interesting advertisement dull. Real interest will induce a reader to read longer copy, word by word, whereas the lack of it will not induce him to read even shorter copy.

When Shorter? When Longer?

What specific factors will help you decide which length copy will do the best job? When longer? When shorter? How much longer or shorter? There can be no scientifically absolute answers to these questions. But certain factors, when carefully weighed against each other, will guide you to the wisest decision humanly possible. Some of these factors are:

1. Type of product
2. Size of space
3. Your objective for that advertisement
4. Price of product
5. Where advertisement is appearing
6. Inherent power of appeal of product or idea behind it
7. Type of advertiser
8. Competition
9. Type of readership you want
10. Appearance of advertisement

1. WHICH TYPE OF PRODUCT?

Concerning No. 1: Type of product advertised has a close relationship to length of copy most effective in selling it. As the late researcher Dr. L. D. H. Weld said, "Advertising is a part of the selling process. When advertising is used, less personal salesmanship is necessary. Advertising supplants personal salesmanship—partially for some commodities; substantially in the case of others, such as certain drug and grocery items; completely in the case of mail-order selling."

Therefore, decide first how much of your dependence upon at-the-counter salesmanship you want your advertising to supplant. Then ask yourself: Is the product an impulse item? Is it in the daily-necessity class? Is it a cheap, casual purchase—such as a bar of candy or a stick of gum? If your answer to any of these questions is yes, then the copy may be shorter than if the answer is no. In the latter case, longer selling copy is indicated. In either case, your conclusion must also be predicated upon other perhaps counterbalancing factors—such as competition, price comparison, and others to be discussed.

Also, if the type of product requires that the idea behind it (or the desirability of utilizing its general function) must be introduced to the reader, then greater copy length will be needed than if the product and/or its function are known and accepted.

2. HOW MUCH SPACE?

Many full pages are filled with messages that belong in half pages, quarter pages, or single columns—and vice versa. To guard against excessive space units it is, when possible, not a bad idea to do as mail-order people do—decide what space you need to do the desired job, then buy it—rather than buy the space and then decide what to put into it. If the decision as to space size is up to you, ask yourself: How *little* space can I use to do the same or a better job?—and remember that a small space unit is a challenge, not an insult.

To determine the copy length to use in your space, the safe procedure (for reasons previously outlined) is to use as much copy as you can, without sacrificing attention-getting and attention-holding power. In full pages the copy blocks can be sizeable, without risking this sacrifice.

3.   WHAT'S YOUR OBJECTIVE?

The farther you want to propel your reader along the road to a completed sale, the more copy you will need.

If the advertiser insists that "We advertise to create an impression, not to make the reader do something," then the copy job is easier—and shorter. Also, if you can tell your copy story in a few words and still get the degree of action you want, do it. Or if writing "reminder advertising," your copy can be shorter; but bear in mind that adding a little more copy can often make such advertising get action from some of your readers, besides conveying a reminder to the others.

4.   HOW MUCH DOES THE PRODUCT COST?

The higher the price the more copy you are likely to need in order to get immediate action—unless a follow-up method makes up the deficit. There is a quantitative "arithmetic of words" that is independent of the selling quality of the words themselves. A salesman will require fewer words to sell an inexpensive suit than to sell a more expensive suit of the same make. The person who is trying to borrow money from a friend will have to use more words when seeking $100 than when going after only $10. As previously mentioned, advertisers who can check results accurately find a close relationship between the amount they are trying to get and the number of words necessary to get it.

Also significant is the remark, "There must be something to it, to be able to talk that much about it." This remark, regardless of the price of your product, does not justify mere prolixity, for tons of words can never take the place of good sales ideas. Yet (aside from that necessity) the words in an advertisement do, cumulatively, have an effect upon people—*if,* despite its length, the copy continues to hold their interest.

5.   WHERE WILL THE ADVERTISEMENT APPEAR?

Obviously, it is logical for copy appearing in newspapers to be shorter than copy for the same product in magazines. Newspapers get a quicker reading and have a shorter life than magazines. But good weekly magazine sections of newspapers are comparable to good weekly magazines.

Nevertheless, copy in newspapers, even in small space, need not be made so short that it is unable to do a good selling job. Before us is a meat packer's advertisement about the deliciousness of smoked tongue. It measures 146 lines, 73 lines by 2 columns. One hundred and two lines are devoted to an excellent headline with adequate white space, a luscious picture of a platter of tongue, a clear reproduction of the trade-mark. Yet in the remaining space of only 44 lines are set 166 words of persuasive, action-getting copy.

6.   THE MOST POWERFUL FACTOR OF ALL

No. 6, Inherent power of the appeal of the product or the idea behind it: This is the most powerful of all factors governing your decision as to the most effective copy length. If the product and its appeal are absolute naturals in themselves, then shorter (or short) copy is all you need; and many of the other factors suggested here are either modified or nullified. But be very sure it really is a "pushover product"; that doesn't occur often.

On the other hand, the weaker this inherent appeal, the more copy (filled with best possible sales angles) you will need. This No. 6 factor not only affects the quantity of copy but also its quality. For example, I would much rather bet upon the effectiveness of an ad selling a product whose basic appeal is so exceptionally powerful that it shines through even poor-quality copy than I would upon the ability of even superlative-quality copy in selling a product with an inherently weak basic appeal. One great writer of advertising, Joe Katz, put it this way: "You can't kill a big idea by bad workmanship." And one writer about advertising, William H. Whyte, Jr., spells it out by saying ". . . If a theme is a strong one it takes a tremendous amount of bad writing to keep it from coming through."

7.   TYPE OF ADVERTISER?

His attitude has the most important bearing of all upon your decision as to the best copy length. If his wall motto, regardless of consequences, is "Make It Short!" your biggest selling job is ahead of you. (And you may get some silent consolation out of Howard G. Sawyer's remark: "Long copy doesn't scare away readers the way it scares away advertisers.")

8.   HOW STIFF IS YOUR COMPETITION?

Weigh the effects of "greater copy length and more fully sold readers" as an antidote to brand switching; unfavorable price comparison; apathetic co-operation from retailers on display material and other promotional activities; or your product's trailing position behind the leaders.

Some advertisers rely almost entirely upon "reminder advertising" to keep their products moving. In composite form here is their reasoning:

"All I want to do is keep the name of my product before the public. After all, it is a leader in its field; has wide general acceptance, distribution, sale; is in the daily-necessity class; is priced right, competitively. I just have to keep reminding people of its name!"

Such reasoning is common, but is it safe? In a competitive market (and how few are not!) sublime reliance upon reminder advertising allows another, and perhaps smaller, operator a chance to come through with advertising that really sells. And with this action-producing copy he may cash in heavily on the public acceptance already created for that *type* of product by those now relying on reminders.

How often we have all seen leaders become followers because they "coasted along on their names"; while followers (or even utter new-comers in the field) became leaders because they put, and kept, the selling pressure on.

Brash newcomers seldom exhibit the expected reverence for the position of long-established leaders in their field. Some of them have managed to cut the ground right from under these leaders—by using strong-selling advertising that not only conveys a reminder to all of its readers, but also converts, and gets action from, many of them.

9.   WHAT TYPE OF READERSHIP?

Don't imagine that the higher the quality of readership you want, the less you need copy with plenty of selling in it.

The quality of the readership you want does not impose a penalty upon copy length. If it is interesting copy and they are human beings, your longer copy will be read. And it is needed, even to sell quality prospects. (As mentioned before, have you ever noticed that richer people are usually more careful buyers, need even more facts and persuasion than poorer ones?)

10.   WHAT ABOUT APPEARANCE?

Requirements as to this may, in some measure, limit copy length to less than you decide is really advisable. If the advertiser prefers, and is satisfied with, aesthetic beauty—rather than greater results—that is his right. However, the suggestions already made can help you use copy of the length you deem necessary and still keep the appearance of the advertisement attractive.

And Now You're Going to Cut—or to Expand

Your consideration of these ten circumstances and limitations will aid you in determining the copy length most practicable for any particular job. It will also help you decide how to cut or expand your garment of words in order to clothe your assigned copy job with the greatest possible *resultfulness*. And it will also help you choose what sales appeals must without fail be pieced into this garment; which rate major emphasis; which may safely be relegated to minor position in the copy story; which may with least risk be left out entirely.

The success of your copy requires that you know as much as possible about the true worth of these sales angles and the relative order of their persuasiveness in advertising that product. Every sales angle of strong or wide appeal that copy cutting or lack of knowledge causes you to omit (or to stress inadequately) involves a consequent loss of its specific effect upon all your readers in general . . . and, in particular, upon those readers who might have been more influenced by that sales angle than by any others. The stronger the sales point so treated, the greater the resultant loss of its potential effectiveness.

The adequate presentation of a sales angle of perhaps hitherto unrealized potency may require only a few extra sentences or a short paragraph. Often such an angle can give the final sales push to thousands of people whom the rest of the copy has left on the fence. In some cases it alone has meant the difference between the greatest possible success and a lesser degree of success or the total failure of an advertisement; yes, of even a complete campaign.

Here is what happened when a sales angle was left out of three department store advertisements, and out of a proprietary:

1. One advertisement for rubber sheeting said, "Do as hospitals do; protect your bed." It produced $8,300 in sales. An advertisement without this phrase produced $5,000 in sales.

2. An advertisement for men's shorts did twice as well when this single phrase was included: "The grip-fasteners won't pop off."

3. One advertisement for Christmas tree lights mentioned that if one bulb burned out the others on the string would stay lit. It sold 28,000 units. Another advertisement not mentioning this fact sold 7,500 units.

4. Eighteen unsuccessful advertisements of a well-known tonic were transformed into highly profitable ones by the addition of one short paragraph containing 36 words in 7-point type. Carl Byoir,

who handled the expenditure of over $4,000,000 in tested copy for this advertiser (they made shelf-count tests of 1,860 different advertisements within a period of 10 years!) tells us about it: "This paragraph supplied the necessary believable *'reason why'* without which *the very same* advertisements were failures. It read: 'Without iron in your blood nothing you eat does you any good; your food simply passes through you. It is the iron in your blood that enables you to get the good out of your food.' "

You Need This Additional Guidance

Now, specifically, how can you learn more about the relative values of different sales angles; which must be covered fully, regardless of the copy space necessary to do it well; which should be shouted; which can be whispered, if space permits?

You cannot follow your own opinion alone, because copywriters have often found that products aren't always *bought* for what they're *sold* for; that people may be buying a product for reasons and purposes they have discovered for themselves; and that these most telling sales angles (some as seemingly obvious as those which were left out of the advertisement just cited) had not even been put into the copy at all, or had been told in a whisper when they really rated a shout.

Therefore—your own judgment, experience, imagination, and selling instinct should be augmented by:

1. Personal contact, review of correspondence with consumers; consumer-research reports; dealer surveys; actual shelf-count results; retail sales clerk check-ups. (Such studies not only uncover strong sales angles and their relative values but also reveal, for your own copy purposes, the actual words and expressions customers use when referring to the product and to the appeal it has *for them*.)

2. Whatever figures and data you have, or can get, as to the true stature of effectiveness of sales angles featured in previous advertisements or campaigns.

THE LOWLY SUBHEAD

We all know that it is a tough job to get people to read the body matter of an ad with any degree of thoroughness. Readership ratings tell us that the easy-to-read captions under pictures often get a percentage of readership 3 to 10 times greater than that of the "read most" figure achieved by the body matter itself. In fact, the difference is sometimes larger than that.

Yet we do want people to read as much of our body matter as we can entice them to read. Now, aside from doing a better job in the *writing* of this body matter, how can we get people into it more readily, and get them to stay with it longer? That question brings us to our subject, "The Lowly Subhead." Surprisingly, considering its importance, little has been written about it.

IT CAN HOLD YOUR READERS LONGER

Subheads are like ladder rungs which make it easier and more inviting for the reader to keep going down through more of the body matter of an advertisement. The weaker and fewer the rungs the more likely he is to drop beyond any further interest in continuing his readership association with your message.

Now, here are some specific reasons why you should pay more attention to your subheads—and also some suggestions on how to make them do a better job in helping to get your body matter read more thoroughly.

First, subheads are (or can be) much more than merely a means of breaking up body matter physically. They can really be "booster stations" of power and interest. You know how, in electricity, a booster station takes up the current that is transmitted to it, amplifies it to greater strength and power, then sends it on to the next station. Finally, a sequence of these booster stations builds the current up so tremendously that it is able to do the big work demanded of it by the hook-up at the very end of the line.

Subheads can perform a similar function in an ad. That is, the right kind can . . . but not if their true importance is not fully recognized; not if they are not forced to go to work; not if they are merely sprinkled in casually for mechanical "break-up" purposes, almost as an afterthought.

They can do a job, and a big one. But they have to be made "part of the plot" for getting an ad read more completely, for a longer distance, and for a greater period of time. They have to be integrated into the plan and context of the advertisement. Too often they are either eliminated entirely or are stuck in almost as filler, "orphans" that are dropped into their homes *after* the ad is written instead of *when* it is planned and *while* it is being written.

WHY YOU NEED THEM

Let us now get down to some specifics. Since so many ads don't use subheads at all—suppose we first consider why they should:

1. Your object is to keep your reader with you as long as possible, to get him through as much of your body matter as you can.

Subheads will make your body matter look more inviting, less formidable; will help you get more of it read; enable it to achieve a higher "read most" rating. Lots of ads with low ratings in this category could step up this percentage greatly, merely by the use of subheads.

2. Short body matter: even ads with just four or five paragraphs of open, well-displayed body matter can use one or two subheads to advantage. Don't fool yourself on this score. A study of a quantity of readership figures will give you an unpleasant surprise as to how very quickly people's attention and interest wane. Subheads will help you to hold them.

3. Long body matter: a main top subhead of three or four lines, indented (as a secondary headline) can act as a link between the headline and the body matter—heightening interest and bridging the gap between the two.

Many readers, although intrigued by the headline, quickly cool off at the sight of long body matter following. A linking top subhead can increase their interest in what the body matter is going to tell them, and can entice them into the first paragraph of it. (Then also use plenty of short subheads throughout the copy itself.)

How to Make Them Do More Work

How can you make your subheads do a better job? How can you make them an *active* force in your ad, booster stations which excite, amplify, and motivate interest? Here are a few suggestions:

1. Don't wait too long to introduce your first subhead. Some ads run three or four paragraphs before exhibiting their first one.

Two short opening paragraphs and then your first subhead is not a bad rule to observe. Again I suggest that you look at some readership figures; you will get a shock at how very quickly interest lags—and you've lost your reader!

2. If your body matter is pretty long and (for the reasons set forth above) you are using a main top subhead as a sort of secondary headline, tie the *first* phrase of it up, definitely and directly, with the idea or promise of the headline itself. Then, in the *last* phrase of it, put in some good specific "come hither."

Make this secondary headline point the way to the promise of consumer benefits, helpful information, satisfaction of curiosity, entertainment, or news which the body matter itself is going to offer the reader. Such promises of specific, soon-to-be-given information help to get readers into the body matter itself.

Use Questions—Sequence

3. Make some of your subheads interrogative in form—to excite curiosity and interest in the body matter which follows. Ask a question to which people will want to read the answer. Avoid declarative subheads that answer themselves—that don't lead anywhere. Start some with interesting questions beginning with Why, When, How, Which, How Much, etc.

4. In some ads you can make your subheads progressively sequential in character, a kind of Sequential Subhead Synopsis of the sales story which the body matter tells more fully. This helps to keep your

reader with you through the entire body matter; aids in energizing the ad as a "vehicle" for carrying the reader toward the action you want him to take.

5. Integrate your subheads into the plan and context of the copy. Don't virtually sprinkle them out of a shaker after the ad is written. They are closely knit links between your presentations of buying reasons. They are there to advance the copy story, not as static, mechanical devices of mere punctuation.

6. Sometimes you can use subheads in a form which will convey, in display, most of your principal sales points. In this form they provide a synopsized sales story which will get across to glancers, who do not read any more of your ad than this quick-flash epitomization.

7. Some subheads reiterate in capsule form the information already given in the preceding paragraph of the body matter. That doesn't get you anywhere. Instead, make each subhead capsulize the "news lead" of what the next paragraph or section of the body matter is going to reveal to the reader. Lead him on with subheads that move forward.

Let Them Speak Out Strongly

8. Make your subheads stand out physically. Set them larger than, and in a face of type which is different from, that used for the body matter. If they don't stand out from your body matter you defeat one of your purposes—which is to break up that matter and thus make it look more inviting to read.

Your other purpose in using subheads is to hold and amplify interest. But if they don't stand out physically they can't flag the reader's attention and thus win any opportunity to capture and build up his interest.

9. Don't worry too much about the fact that using subheads liberally, and displaying them prominently enough to make them worth using, may make your ad look a little more spotty, unsymmetrical, or inartistic.

Remember, you are not creating a work of art. You are creating a work of business. You are trying to get your copy read more thoroughly so that it will do a better selling job.

It should now be obvious to you that subheads may seem lowly merely because so little has ever been written about them. Actually, when well planned and liberally used, they can be a more powerful factor in an advertisement than you may have ever fully realized.

QUIZ ON CHAPTER 6

1. What are the eight milestones to a sale?

2. Review the twenty-five important words which define the relationship between holding interest longer and making more sales.

3. Name ten of the twenty-two methods suggested for holding interest longer.

4. Name three of the seven ways mentioned for making the body matter in an advertisement *look* more inviting.

5. Review the ten factors that will help you decide which length copy will do the best job.

6. Which is the most powerful factor of all?

7. How safe is it to depend upon "reminder advertising"?

8. What additional guidance do you need in order to select your most irresistible sales angles?

9. Why are subheads so necessary?

10. Cite four of the nine ways suggested for making them do more, and better, work.

AIDA OR EMMA?—WHICH SHALL THE COPYWRITER MARRY?

AIDA is, of course, that well known, four-virtued, psychological soul-mate of copywriters: *Attention, Interest, Desire,* and *Action.* EMMA is a contraction of the initials of that new and more glamorous siren, *Motivation Research*. She probes into the innermost recesses of the lives of those she wishes to influence—from womb to tomb, from foetus to finis.

Which shall today's copywriter marry? Or shall he commit bigamy? Like most maidens, both have faults and virtues. Yet each is inclined to feel that her particular charms are the only ones worthy of the attentions of those who woo her.

AIDA, for example, seems to work somewhat on the assumption that those she tries to influence have minds that are *tabula rasa*—blank tablets unaffected by their previous experiences in life, waiting to record indelibly the message she wishes to impress upon them.

She likes to think that people are quite rational, that the entreaties which she utters so sequentially, so appealingly, are the one best way to invoke the desired response. She has little sympathy with semantics, for she is suspicious of the idea that the connotations of words have been molded or reshaped by the varying experiences of the people who read them.

Now, EMMA seems quite as disdainful of reason and rationalism alone as AIDA is of psychic symbolism alone. She knows that people cannot be divorced from their backgrounds, that they don't come plunk up against an ad without bringing to it a mélange of fixations, fealties and frustrations. And she'll go to almost any extreme to prove that the influence of these must condition every appeal to your mind, your heart, your soul or your pocketbook.

Shall the copywriter go steady with AIDA or with EMMA? Both have some good points and both have some bad points. (As is pointed out here, obviously with some exaggeration and oversimplification, in order to delineate some of their differences more sharply.)

No, AIDA does not believe too much in basing the ad on the id. Her favorite approach (even though it may contain plenty of emotional appeal) is a nice tidy one—a logical 1, 2, 3, 4 for people who will read the *complete* advertisement, act rationally, and do what they are asked to do. She likes all her arguments to be linked in a shipshape way so that they will bring her reading, viewing, or listening passengers safe into port.

EMMA, on the other hand, can be just as much of an extremist as AIDA. She's very alluring, that one. Sometimes it seems as though sex and its symbols are in sole control of her whole existence. She can hardly look at a potato without wondering whether its eyes are turned lasciviously upon her. Her probings into motivation dig not only into the infancy of the interviewee but into his prenatal influences—yea, verily, beyond that and back into the vagaries of his ancestors. (Was your grandmother ever frightened into hysteria by a mad dog? How obvious it is that you will shrink from the purchase of a dog biscuit whose label pictures an old lady feeding that brand to her dog!)

In an attempt to merge their virtues and submerge their faults for his own purposes, it looks as though the good copywriter will have to become a bigamist. And, being doubly married, he'll have to be a doubly good husband and listen a bit to the advice of both. He'll have to use the mundane check list provided by AIDA as well as the more celestial navigation provided by EMMA.

And, when you come to think of it, isn't that what most of the real top-notch copywriters have always done? Before EMMA was ever invited into the advertising world, weren't the great copy geniuses (the Getchells, Seagroves, Bartons, the Claude Hopkins, Ray Rubicams, Jim Youngs, and Wilbur Ruthrauffs) freewheeling *instinctively* along at least *part* of EMMA Avenue?

For example, a book by Martin Mayer (*Madison Avenue, U.S.A.*) points out that it is astonishing how often "motivational analyses lead to copy suggestions which a first-class advertising man should have found without any Freudian explanation." (That's in EMMA's department.) And it also points out that many other proposals could have come out of one of the "primers for students in advertising courses." (That's in AIDA's department.)

However, since so few of us are Getchells *et al.,* I imagine that we should give one ear each to the blandishments of both AIDA and EMMA—and thus try to achieve by industry and intent some measure of the accomplishment which our greatest copywriting geniuses so often achieved by instinct and inspiration.

CHAPTER 7

HOW TO GET MORE INQUIRIES

Many firms run advertising whose purpose is to produce inquiries to be sent by prospective customers directly to the advertiser. Getting such inquiries is a highly important and necessary part of their business operations.

These advertisers are not in the mail-order business. The inquiries brought by their advertising are followed up by their own salesmen or by those of their dealers or distributors. Or they are answered by sales literature alone—literature designed to induce these prospects to purchase the product entirely on their own initiative at a retail outlet.

Inquiries—the Cornerstone of Many Businesses

Millions of dollars are spent on such advertising. Since getting a sufficient quantity of inquiries is so vital to so many firms, perhaps the information given in this chapter will be useful. Additional suggestions are given which can improve the quality of inquiries, and help to develop a type of coupon which will aid in accomplishing both of these purposes.

The subject of this book is the writing of copy for *all* types of advertising. Therefore, although some mail-order advertisers pull for inquiries, the guidance given in the book is not solely applicable to them. As previously stated, many general advertisers pull for inquiries . . . and obtaining good ones at a satisfactory price is a cornerstone of their business. Pulling for direct *orders* is not discussed at all: that is the province of the mail-order advertiser entirely.

133

Ten Ways to Increase Them

Of course, the quantity of inquiries which any advertisement can produce is basically dependent upon the appeal of the article advertised and of the offer which is made. However, there are certain ways to increase quantity, or to decrease it, at will. Let us first discuss ten of the many ways to increase it.

1. If offering a free booklet, you may give it a title which promises the prospect useful information in addition to the selling talk about your product. This information must of course appear in the booklet and should be directly related to your product's function.

[*For example*] FIVE SIMPLE WAYS TO CUT YOUR HOME-HEATING COSTS—*instead of* THE STORY OF THE DOUBLE-X OIL BURNER; HOW TO AVOID THE 6 MOST COMMON MISTAKES IN MODERNIZING YOUR KITCHEN—*instead of* THE FACTS ABOUT TRIPLE-Z KITCHENS.

2. If your booklet was written by some authority widely and favorably known in your field (or if you can get some such person to write it), play that fact up. Featuring the name of a recognized expert will draw more replies than using an unknown one or no individual's name at all.

3. Perhaps you can inexpensively add novelty value to what you are offering to inquirers . . . swatch samples, miniature model, kit, specimen policy, color chart, slip sheet or show-through demonstration pages, comparative "before and after" presentation, etc. If it be a booklet, maybe it can present your sales story in a novel way—not through some tricky, nonrelevant device, but to bring out more graphically or persuasively the merits of your product.

[*For example*] A certain dictionary publisher got out a booklet containing simple die-cut pages which provided a unique way to "add a new word every day to your vocabulary." It had novelty value and a sound educational idea behind it. Yet it cost very little more to manufacture than a commonplace booklet. And it was tied up closely with selling copy descriptive of this particular dictionary. The advertising produced inquiries for an average of 17 cents each!

You can imagine how much inquiries would cost if the advertising pulled for an ordinary booklet containing only selling talk about a dictionary. But this advertising sold an idea that people knew would help them to do something they had always wanted to do: improve their vocabularies. And it offered them, without cost, an interesting and practical new way to do it.

Another manufacturer prepared his booklet in the form of an inexpensive "motion-picture flipper" showing his product *in action*. He reduced his inquiry cost to 15 cents each.

4. In describing the booklet in your advertisement, refer to certain specific pages, telling how each can be of practical usefulness to the prospect. By thus detailing some of its contents you can add to its appeal.

[*For example*] You might tell your reader how "Page 3 will explain how quickly and easily you can accomplish thus-and-so. Page 7 shows you two methods of saving time and work when you do this-and-that. Page 15 pictures the wrong ways that can cost you money —and how the right ones can bring you a sizable saving."

Even the chapter titles in the famous Dale Carnegie best seller, *How to Win Friends and Influence People*, were planned with this kind of appeal in mind. Each is actually a persuasive headline in itself. Here are a few of them: The Big Secret of Dealing With People, Six Ways to Make People Like You, An Easy Way to Become a Good Conversationalist, How to Interest People, Making People Glad to Do What You Want.

5. You may feature your offer at the very top of the advertisement, picturing it in display or referring to it in your headline or main subhead.

[*For example*] One such advertisement pulled 1,700 inquiries; yet another (appearing in the same linage and publication) pulled only 975 inquiries. The latter mentioned the offer toward the end of the advertisement. Another advertisement, again featuring the offer at the top, brought 5,000 replies; yet one mentioning it simply in a corner panel toward the bottom pulled only 2,366 replies.

6. The greater display you devote to your offer anywhere in your advertisement, the more inquiries you will receive. Even though you may not play it up in the headline or top areas, prominent "down-stairs" display—either pictorial or textual—will increase the flow of inquiries. (A good display line about the offer—sometimes in the form of a caption white on black—directly above the top rule of the coupon itself is often used.)

7. The more quickly you refer to your offer in the body matter of your advertisement the more likely you are to increase inquiries. The reason is obvious, yet often overlooked.

8. You may use a greater amount of body-matter copy about your offer, in relation to that descriptive of the product itself. More wordage about it, if attractively presented, will increase replies.

If your advertisement is appearing in one of your local newspapers, a desirable addition to your copy will be prominent mention of your company's phone number. (This can be such an inquiry stimulant that it really rates a separate entry in this ten-point listing.)

9. State the name and full address of your company at the end of your advertisement—even though you may also use a coupon which supplies it. American magazines have a sizable amount of "secondary" circulation: people to whom the publication is passed on by its first purchasers. How can such people answer an ad if the coupon has already been clipped and the remainder of the advertisement carries no company name and address?

[*For example*] The secondary circulation of five of the country's top magazines ranges from 2.2 to 5.8 readers for each copy sold.

10. If the inquiry is not to be followed up by a salesman, state that fact clearly in the body matter and in the coupon. This is particularly important if your product is of a type commonly sold through a salesman's follow-up call. Use a phrase like "No salesman will call upon you." Many people will not even inquire about something if they think a salesman or agent will then call upon them.

HOW TO REDUCE THE NUMBER OF INQUIRIES

Let's say that, after careful figuring, you decide it would be wiser to reduce quantity—in order to try to improve the quality of inquiries.

Perhaps your figures prove you are getting too many "free riders" or "curiosity leads," or too many replies from juveniles. If you depend entirely upon printed literature to convert inquiries into sales, perhaps your percentage of conversion is not high enough in relation to costs. Or, if inquiries are being followed up by your salesmen (or if you are turning them over to your dealers or distributors), it may be that their ratio of conversion into sale is too low.

A Delicate Balance

To establish a satisfactory balance between the quality and quantity of inquiries is usually a delicate operation. You cannot use meat-ax techniques to cut them down. Certain procedures—which an advertiser may hopefully imagine will cut quantity "only slightly" and, at the same time, improve quality "tremendously"—seldom work out that way.

Actually, what often happens is that the inquiry response is reduced drastically. As a result, the sales which can finally be made to this seriously depleted quantity CANNOT (even though they may be somewhat higher percentagewise) make up sufficiently for the reduction in potential. They cannot fully offset the loss in the number of your opportunities for at least exposing your complete sales story through follow-up literature or salesmen.

To put it in another way, the quality of the inquiries simply has not been that much improved by the methods used to cut down their quantity. Also, of course, you cannot do anything even to *try* to make sales to inquiries you don't get at all.

What to Decide First

So, before you finally adopt any inquiry-reducing procedures, first be absolutely certain that your inquiries are too poor in quality. You can't be casual, hasty, or "hunchy" about it. You can't depend on guesswork. Too much is at stake—considering that the wastebaskets of American business are each day filled with fortunes in potential profits represented by inquiries which someone has (perhaps quite arbitrarily) decided to be "not worth following up."

You can't judge by handwriting. (Have you ever attempted to read some college-examination papers?) You can't safely judge by the address from which the inquiry comes. These days, Mr. Able To Buy may reside in almost any neighborhood. Nor are salesmen's reports on calls always dependable. A favorite alibi of many incapable salesmen is, "The quality of the lead you gave me was poor."

How to Decide Whether to Reduce Them

What can you do, specifically, to help make a wise decision? Well, if your inquiries are followed up by printed literature only, you can make a split-run test. You can split evenly, into two sizable groups, those inquiries obtained through advertising which utilized quantity-reducing techniques and those which did not. You can use all possible care to see that, except for this one factor, the two groups represent a fair comparison—as to source of inquiry, date received, geographical area, etc.

Then—using the same literature but with two different key numbers to show from which group the replies later come—you can follow up these two groups at the same time.

Your results will indicate which type of inquiry produced the better net for you, and give you valid comparisons as to which can supply you with the more profitable and desirable volume. In your calculations you will likewise have to consider that inquiry-cutting procedures deprive you of names to which you could have sent a whole series of follow-ups. Not being able to do so costs you whatever profits your figures indicate this business would have been worth.

If your inquiries are followed up by salesmen you can devise other testing methods. For instance, before the salesman calls, you may send out an advance "appointment" or other type of mailing to evaluate or to validate the sincerity of the inquiry. Or you may make a test with "call-backs," using salesmen other than those who made the first call. Or you may check back on salesmen's call reports for patterns of performance in their handling of all types of inquiries.

And now suppose that whatever tests you can devise have conclusively demonstrated the advisability of cutting down your inquiries. Unless your advertising went to unjustifiable extremes in pressing for inquiry volume regardless of the worth of the inquiries, you have realized that such tests were necessary in order to reach a sound decision. So now that you've decided about it, what are you going to do? What methods, specifically, are you going to use to reduce quantity in order to try to improve quality? Here are ten you may consider.

Ten Ways to Reduce Them

1. If offering a booklet, you may give it a title indicating that its contents are confined to a description of your product and its merits. (The opposite of the suggestion made in Item No. 1, p. 134.)

2. Your copy can make it clear that the booklet's contents are devoted solely to a sales presentation of your product.

3. You may mention in your copy certain "qualifying" facts—perhaps your product's price, maintenance, or installation costs or requirements, etc. Obviously, the greater the negative influence of the information you give the more you will reduce inquiries. So this procedure, like all the others mentioned in this listing, must be handled judiciously . . . or you will "qualify" your inquiries to the vanishing point.

4. You may reduce the display you devote to what you offer. (The opposite of Item No. 6, p. 136.)

[*For example*] When an advertiser wishes to test the readership of an advertisement he may use an undisplayed and keyed "buried offer" somewhere near the end of the copy. His purpose is not to get quantities of unqualified inquiries. It is to check on how effectively his advertisement has gotten attention and how thoroughly it was read.

5. You may want to take specific steps to cut down the number of inquiries from juveniles.

[*For example*] Your coupon may request the inquirer to state his age. Or you may say something like "This offer must be limited to people over 18 years of age." Such methods can cut down juvenile inquiries but will not of course eliminate them entirely. If the offer is attractive some juveniles will fill in the age of an adult or will ignore the stipulation.

One method used successfully is to print a little check box at the bottom of the coupon. Next to it appears the phrase "If 18 years of age or under check here for Booklet A." This helps to stimulate the desired action because it suggests a possible advantage. Such inquiries can then be handled in a way different from adult ones. More drastic methods of discouraging juvenile inquiries can be employed—and this is particularly important when inquiries are to be followed up by salesmen.

6. You may use a smaller amount of body-matter copy about your offer in relation to that descriptive of the product itself. (The opposite of Item No. 8, p. 136.)

7. The coupon itself may be eliminated, thus requiring a greater amount of effort for the reader to inquire.

8. The coupon may ask the respondent to supply information other than merely his name and address—such as occupation, position, reference, which specific size or model he'd like more information about, stipulation that business card or letterhead be used in replying, etc.

9. You may make your main headline (and the basic content of your copy) more selective and qualifying in its appeal. This major operation will automatically reduce inquiries by restricting readership.

[*For example*] Note the selective elements purposely introduced into these headlines—IF YOUR LAWN MEASURES AT LEAST 100x100 . . . THIS NEW POWER MOWER WAS DESIGNED ESPECIALLY FOR YOU; A PLAN FOR MEN WHO WANT TO RETIRE AT 60 . . . AND CAN START SETTING ASIDE $200 A MONTH FOR IT NOW.

10. You may make a small charge for the booklet about your product. Advertisers sometimes feel that requiring a small token payment (10 cents or 25 cents for instance) will not reduce quantity "too much" but will improve quality so markedly that the increased net sales to these inquiries will more than offset this depletion.

However, it is common for such procedures to cut inquiries by at least 50 per cent, and even up to 80 per cent. Naturally people do not relish having to pay the advertiser even a small amount for sales material designed to induce them to buy his product.

It very frequently works out that making a small charge for your booklet slashes the quantity of inquiries so seriously that even an increased percentage of closure on the inquiries you do receive cannot make up for it. In other words, the inquiries you *don't* get, you of course can't work on at all—and many a reader who *would be* susceptible to a complete sales talk does not inquire and therefore of course never receives it.

[*For example*] Ad A pulled for inquiries for a free booklet. Produced 4,870 inquiries. Nine per cent of these were converted into sales: 438 sales. Ad B was the same in every respect except for requesting 10 cents for postage. It appeared in the same publication. Produced only 2,310 inquiries. Eleven per cent of these were converted into sales: 254 sales. Result: a much greater net profit on Ad A, after accurately apportioned deduction of overhead and cost of initial follow-up and postage. Besides, on Ad A, 4,432 unsold inquiries were left for potential profit through further follow-up. On Ad B only 2,056 unsold inquiries remained.

Whether you decide to take measures to reduce quantity or to increase it will, of course, be finally determined by a considerable amount of careful sharp-pencil arithmetic. That is vital. Among the items in your calculations will be your present cost per inquiry, percentage of conversion into orders, cost per order, follow-up expense (whether by salesmen or by sales literature alone), overhead, spread between manufacturing cost and selling price, optimum volume net collections.

HOW TO MAKE THE INQUIRY COUPON ITSELF DO A BETTER JOB

If your advertisement asks its readers to respond directly to you, perhaps to facilitate that action it ends with a coupon. Does that mean that coupons must remain the merely passive appendages we find in many couponed advertisements? No. Can they be made active producers of increased and more profitable response in themselves? Yes. Specifically how?

Well, first we'll have to consider the appeals and sales arguments which are presented to the reader before he reaches the coupon. In a given advertisement they will naturally *read* the same. But they are *not* the same—in their selling impact upon the minds and emotions of the individual readers of your advertisement.

Three Kinds of Prospects

As explained in Chapter 6, these individual reader prospects of yours will fall into three general classifications: (1) At one extreme are those from whom it will be hardest to get an immediate response— least susceptible to persuasion concerning your particular product. (2) At the other extreme are those from whom it will be the easiest to get an immediate response—most susceptible, because of their current needs or desires and the resultant impact of your sales story. (3) The majority of your readers are between these two extremes. They comprise those who are easier to activate than Group 1, harder than Group 2. These Group 3 prospects can be persuaded to respond—IF the elements in your advertisement, working together, induce them to do so.

One such element can be your coupon; not merely in its passive role of simply facilitating a response but, as will be shown, in the active function of helping to *create* more of them and more profitable ones.

Yes, coupons (the "last word" your advertisement has with your prospects) can be either a depressant or a stimulant in their influence upon responsiveness. Properly planned, they can help tip the scales in your favor and get more replies from hardest-to-activate Group 1; produce a greater volume of replies and more profitable ones per unit from easiest-to-activate Group 2; and increase the responsiveness of those in the in-between Group 3.

Ten Ways to Improve Your Coupon

So now we're on the subject of the coupons themselves. Here are ten of the ways to word them in order to get more and better inquiries.

1. With the coupon alone in mind, review the suggestions given in Items No. 6 and 10, concerning quantity; Items No. 5, 7, 8, concerning quality. (Pages 136 and 140.)

2. In a little panel in the coupon offer an additional inducement for quick response. Due to human inertia and other factors of attrition, the more quickly you can get the bulk of your inquiries from a publication, the greater will be the final total response.

> [*For example*] One tax service selling through salesman uses a coupon which pulls for inquiries for a free booklet—but a little coupon panel offers to include with it a Supplementary Tax Report to those who mail the coupon promptly.

3. For the same reason as above, mention in your coupon any other factual circumstance justifying, and stimulating, a quicker response. (See Chapter 5, *Ask for Action*.) Such motivating factors can be so influential as to deserve prominent coverage in other parts of the advertisement too.

> [*For example*] A few such circumstances might be that the price of your product is scheduled to go up, or has just been reduced, or a certain model of it is in limited supply, or is available for only a limited time, etc.

4. Work into the body of the coupon itself a little persuasive copy about the value and usefulness of what you are going to send free.

5. Word your coupon so that it first tells what the inquirer is going to get; then, if any requirement at all has to be met, what he has to do

to get it. Stress the fact that "mailing the coupon involves no further obligation," if such is the case.

6. If you also have a Canadian address from which replies can be serviced, state it at the bottom of the coupon. Many American magazines have sizable circulations in Canada—and people naturally prefer to do business in their own country and with a firm nearer to them.

[*For example*] The Canadian circulation of four of the largest American magazines ranges from 4 per cent to 10 per cent—a percentage well worth this little line.

Also, if you have several offices (located, for instance, in our own East, Midwest or Pacific areas) the response to your national advertising can be increased by putting these addresses in the coupon.

7. Increase response by wording the coupon so that it points out the specific benefits which may be obtained through the use of your product or service.

[*For example*] One institution uses a coupon which contains a check list itemizing the specific advantages provided by its product. This type of coupon emphasizes and brings right down into the coupon itself, the strongest of the various appeals elaborated upon in the rest of the advertisement.

8. The value of an inquiry may be "traded up" by using in the coupon a check box and a little rider in which is briefly described a larger size, or more expensive, model of the product being advertised.

9. Also possessing trading-up potentialities similar to those mentioned above is the type of coupon which has two objectives. Again through check boxes, it seeks to broaden the general appeal of the advertisement and also (different from No. 8, p. 140) to induce the prospect to inquire about one or more additional and related products.

[*For example*] One manufacturer's advertising is based upon the pleasure and profit of having one's own home workshop. The coupon check-lists a number of different power tools about which literature will be sent. The advertising of a home-study institution (whose inquiries are followed up by salesmen) sells the general idea of more pay through self-improvement. Its coupon check-lists the particular courses available.

Two other schools base their advertising upon the desirability of learning a foreign language and of learning to play a musical instrument. Their coupons give a check list of the languages and the musical instruments for which they offer courses.

This type of advertising no. only interests more people by broadening the appeal; it also trades up the value of the coupons themselves by eliciting inquiries about more than one product. It could be used profitably by more advertisers than now employ it.

10. Inquiries may be automatically increased by removing obstructions to your reader's immediate action. Any factors (even seemingly minor ones) which make it harder, or less convenient, for him to respond *at once*—or those which tend to confuse or make him indecisive —will cut down coupon response.

That means, among many other things, coupons with as much fill-in space as practicable; company names and addresses preferably short and simple; a clearly worded presentation of an attractive offer; and coupons which, physically, have an invitingly uncomplicated appearance.

It is not easy to get people to notice an advertisement, then to induce them to read it through, and finally to go through the various steps necessary to mail a response. So anything you can think of which will make it less of a chore for them to take that final action at once will, of itself, increase the number (and the value) of the coupons you will receive.

COUPON RIDERS—WORTH MUCH, COST LITTLE OR NOTHING

As just briefly mentioned, the value of an inquiry coupon to the advertiser may be greatly increased by the use of a checker-box rider in the coupon. Riders are simply last-minute "hitchhikers" designed to take advantage, *to the fullest possible extent,* of the favorable reaction which the advertisement as a whole may have generated.

Instead of holding all readers down to one level of response, the purpose of these riders is to induce them to take more than the minimum degree of action requested in the main body of your coupon or advertisement. By offering an extra inducement—or merely through the power of suggestion—coupon riders give to those who are most susceptible to the appeal of your advertisement (Groups 2 and 3, mentioned in Chapter 6) an opportunity to "let themselves go."

As you can readily see, riders can thus be tremendously important in increasing the ultimate profitability of an advertisement. In fact, the percentage of readers who accept the offer or suggestion made in a good rider is often so sizable (sometimes 40 per cent, or even more) as to turn a high cost-per-inquiry into a satisfactory one.

And remember: Using a short rider in the coupon may cost you nothing extra for linage. It can usually be worked in at the bottom of a coupon without increasing the size of an advertisement.

Allow People to Trade Up If They Want to

Of course, mail-order advertisers use riders for many purposes: for example, to produce orders for a more expensive model; to offer a saving on a multiple order; to get cash in advance; to offer an inducement involving a saving to the respondent of postage and shipping costs; or to get an additional order for a different, but related, product.

However, advertisers who pull for inquiries but are not in the mail-order business can likewise use riders profitably. A worth-while percentage of those who read their advertisements will be interested in trading up. So they will mark the check box requesting information, for example, about a more expensive model of the product advertised, or some related product. They may be willing to take voluntary action of some kind to make those particular coupons more valuable to the advertiser. In other words, although it may be wise to feature in the advertisement the least expensive model of a product, the inquiry coupon need not hold responses down to that level of reponse.

To sum up on the subject of coupons: Your advertisement pulling for inquiries can be persuasive in every other respect; but you won't cash in on the full measure of this unless its final word (the coupon) gathers up and delivers to the advertiser all the inquiry-producing power which the advertisement has "fired up." Many an inquiry advertisement whose copy kindles "shoot-the-works" fire in the minds and emotions of its readers ends up with a type of coupon which snuffs this flame back to a flicker.

SEVEN OTHER FACTORS WHICH INFLUENCE THE EFFECTIVENESS OF AN ADVERTISEMENT

Whether or not an advertisement is pulling for inquiries, certain factors (apart from the content of the advertisement itself) have a major influence on how well it accomplishes the purpose you have set for it. Many of these factors you can do something about in advance, others you cannot. Here are some of them.

Size of Advertisement

Naturally its size has a vital bearing on how much attention an advertisement will get and, if pulling for inquiries, how many it will bring. Concerning the latter, it is a mistake to assume that large-space advertisements will produce increased inquiries in direct proportion to their size. For example, experience indicates that a full-page advertisement will not bring twice as many inquiries as a half page; it is more likely to produce about two-thirds as many more inquiries.

The Use of Color

The addition of color will increase attention value and inquiry pull. A four-color advertisement will often bring about 50 per cent more inquiries than the same one in black and white. However, this is a matter to be weighed carefully—because the rate charged for the use of color is sometimes entirely out of proportion to the increased direct response it can possibly bring or the greater attention it is likely to attract.

One of the principal factors in your decision will be whether your advertisement, or the pictorial display of the product, really *requires* the use of color for optimum effectiveness, regardless of its cost.

When It Appears

You can automatically assure more effectiveness for your advertisements if you run them when people are devoting more time to the publications they read and when newsstand circulations are less subject to the usual seasonal drop-off. *This presupposes that your product does not have a strong seasonal appeal which requires that your advertising coincide with it.*

You must, of course, pay the full rate whether your advertisement appears in an April or a May issue or in a January or February one. Yet the newsstand circulation of a publication may drop off as much as 40 per cent for the April or May issues as compared with the January or February ones. In that case you are paying 100 per cent of the rate for 60 per cent of the circulation.

Also, the actual readership of publications varies greatly throughout the year. This is due to the reading habits of people and the various attractions competing for their time and activities. Time is not expandable, it is merely expendable. And we expend more time on sports, travel, the use of our cars, television, radio, and other interests during some months of the year than we do in others. That (with a certain amount of offset due to our now having more leisure hours in general) leaves us less time for reading our publications.

The voluminous records kept by advertisers who seek a direct and immediate response to their advertising show that their five most effective months are January, February, September, October, and November—that is, from publications actually *appearing* in those months, regardless of the "cover date" of the publication. April and May are usually the poorest, as much as 50 per cent down compared with January.

Therefore, if the nature of the advertiser's business permits it and if his product need not be tied up with a seasonal appeal at variance with this recommendation, consider concentrating more of your advertising during months when the circulations of publications are at their peak, when they are best read, and when the normal human inertia and lassitude which all advertisers must fight to overcome are more actively offset by the stimulus of invigorating weather and less subject to the readership-killing temptations of the outdoors.

Position

The position of an advertisement in a publication is of major importance—particularly in these times when so many other interests compete for the time which readers may devote to perusing publications and advertising. Yet much space is bought without any consideration whatever as to what position the advertisement will occupy—*except* by advertisers who keep keyed records and know that the factor of position alone can mean the difference between the success or failure of an advertisement.

These advertisers make every effort to obtain right-hand pages rather than left-hand ones, with the exception of certain special positions as will later be mentioned. Perhaps it is not irrelevant to mention that surveys show that, after entering a retail store, twice as many people will normally swing to the right rather than to the left. Based upon the experience of such advertisers (and who else has more meaningful statistical evidence?), here is a guide to the relative effectiveness of various positions in the magazines:

> *For Full-Page Space:* The back cover comes first. The right-hand page, facing the inside front cover, comes next; that would be page 1 or page 3, depending on how the magazine numbers its pages. Then any one of the next five right-hand pages, *the farther forward the better*. Then the left-hand page facing the third cover. The page opposite the table of contents is often desired because of increased reader traffic.
>
> The second cover (inside front cover) and third cover (inside back cover) are good positions for general advertisers—but advertisers who pull for a direct response do not use second covers because readers hesitate to deface the front cover in order to tear out a coupon.

For Columns or Smaller Space: It depends on how far back in the magazine you must go in order to secure a right-hand position. Better to be well forward on the left-hand page than too far in the rear on a right-hand page.

An advertisement on a left-hand page opposite four or five columns of editorial matter is preferable to a right-hand position with other advertisers sharing the page and the facing page. Top of outside column on a right-hand page, as far forward in the magazine as possible, is a much-sought position.

Obviously, the matter of good position is even more important for advertisements of a size which cannot acquire any domination by virtue of large space alone. The problems of smaller-than-page-space advertisers have been somewhat ameliorated by many magazines through improved editorial make-up which, through story carryovers, distributes reader interest throughout an entire issue, from cover to cover.

Careful space buying can increase the resultfulness of any advertisement, large or small. Good position wins for page space a bigger percentage of readership—and can make even small space do a better job than larger units which are very poorly positioned.

The Effect of Big News Events

If a news event of sufficient magnitude occurs simultaneously with the appearance of an advertisement pulling for inquiries, it can play havoc with its resultfulness. This is something that the advertiser can do nothing about; but after "the roof falls in" he can at least know why it happened.

I have had many such experiences over the years, going all the way back to 1932. The kidnaping of the Lindbergh baby happened in March of that year. For weeks this event captured most of the readership of the newspapers and this concentration drastically depleted the readership of the magazines. The volume of inquiries in one case dropped 51 per cent as compared with an insertion of the same advertisement appearing in the same newspaper one month before the kidnaping; in one of the weekly magazines the inquiries dropped 70 per cent; in four national monthlies, 30 per cent.

The beginning of the German attack on Poland on September 1, 1939, caused a drop of 34 per cent in the inquiry results from monthly magazines. The German invasion of the Netherlands and Belgium caused a drop of 36 per cent, 48 per cent, and 71 per cent in three publications checked, two of them monthlies.

Of course, it goes without saying that a fortuitous news break relating to the field in which your product plays a part can do just the opposite, stimulating inquiries tremendously.

The Effect of Weather

Weather is another factor about which Mark Twain said you can do nothing. But at least you can know its *effect* upon the production of inquiries. Some years ago I made an analysis of the 57,000 inquiries received from 84 different insertions appearing during an eleven-year period. The proposition being advertised was the same; so was the position used and the publication, the back cover of a Sunday section of one of the New York City newspapers.

I checked back on the weather reports for these 84 Sundays, correlated them with the inquiry figures. The result: 19 percent more inquiries were received when the weather (due to rain, sleet, or snow) was such as to discourage those pursuits which competed with the reading of the newspaper. And this despite the fact that it might be assumed that on some of these bad days exceedingly inclement weather might have caused some decrease in the newsstand sales of the newspaper. No wonder that advertisers who pull for a direct response (except retail stores, *of course*) pray for rain when they have an expensive newspaper advertisement running on a given day!

And the Most Important Factor of All

Most important of all factors for advertisers who want their copy to produce more inquiries, and better ones, is the keeping of accurate records of the resultfulness of each keyed advertisement. Doing this systematically, diligently, and over a period, will cut down costly mistakes and will tell you:

> *Which* publications to continue using, which to drop out of; which pull inquiries of good quality, which poor; where to get the greatest, and most profitable, volume; and where most quickly.
>
> *Whether* to use daily newspapers during the week or to use Sunday ones when people have more time to read and to respond; which specific pages or sections; which days of the week give you better results; or whether, on the other hand, it is better to use weekly magazines or monthlies.
>
> *When* to run and how often.
>
> *What* positions are best in each publication.
>
> *Which* advertisements should be retained, which discarded; should the offer itself be changed, perhaps offering a different incentive for stimulating inquiries?
>
> *What* elements differentiate them, so that you can incorporate the salient elements of the successful advertisements into new ones, avoid in the future whatever elements are commonly present in the unsuccessful ones.
>
> *When* to repeat the same advertisement in the same publication and when to use a different one; how long an interim is wise before repetition. (The percentage of drop-off in result due to repetition varies greatly by publication.)
>
> *Which* publications are giving you a diminishing return because of circulation being piled on by methods involving such an abnormally low subscription price that you may be paying for quantity of circulation alone, without regard for the quality and thoroughness of readership.
>
> *Where,* as to the part of the country or which economic level, your best results are coming from.

In these and other ways, accurate records can provide priceless guidance in increasing the quantity, and improving the quality, of inquiries. Those whose advertising procedures can produce such records of response, and whose selling procedures can utilize them, are indeed fortunate. Not to employ this information to the full extent of its great potential profitability is an arrant, although not uncommon, waste of opportunity.

QUIZ ON CHAPTER 7

1. Name five of the ten ways suggested for increasing the number of inquiries.

2. How can you decide whether it might actually be more profitable to reduce the quantity of inquiries?

3. Name five of the ten ways suggested for reducing them.

4. Name five of the ten ways suggested for making the copy in the coupon itself work harder.

5. How can coupon riders take fuller advantage of the favorable reaction your entire advertisement has generated?

6. Name seven other factors which influence the effectiveness of an advertisement.

7. Will a full-page advertisement ordinarily produce twice as many inquiries as a half page?

8. Which two months are normally the poorest producers of inquiries?

9. What is the most essential requirement for advertisers who pull for inquiries?

10. Which questions will be answered by the meticulous carrying out of this requirement?

YOU CAN PROFIT—AFTER HOURS

It's the hours you're *not* paid for that can pay you best!
I've just been looking at a chart showing how much one's increased

earnings can total in the course of the years. For example, a $100-per-month increase will total $12,000 in 10 years, $18,000 in 15 years. A $200-a-month increase represents $24,000 in 10 years, $36,000 in 15 years.

Obviously, to the younger copy man the significant message of the chart is: "The sooner in my working years that I can justify these raises, and the more frequently I can telescope them throughout those years, the higher will they total over my working life."

How? Well, at least as far as my own observation goes, not by regular office hours alone. Except for exceptional creative people, office hours—although conscientiously devoted to producing good, acceptable work day after day—will mainly serve to bring regular raises and periodic promotion over the years. To accelerate this pace requires after hours thinking and working.

Suppose we figure it this way: Let's say regular hours mean about 1,715 working hours per year: 49 weeks of 35 hours each. Doing good work, doing assigned jobs satisfactorily, may enable the copy man to advance himself with regularity. But it's not likely to accelerate his pace with the quicker and higher jumps that can total so much more over the full working span of his life—besides being spendable as he goes along.

No, it's afterhours time that can tilt the scales. It's the hours you're not paid for that can pay you best.

Use regular hours for jobs that are assigned, done well. Use after-hours for the extra time that brings the extra reward . . . for brain waves on extracurricular jobs or accounts for which you have not been given assignment slips . . . for special attention or concentration not possible in the hubbub of the office. And, more prosaically, for doing that additional *quantity* of work that somehow begets the ability to do work of superior *quality*. (Have you ever noticed that the most capable of all creative people in literature and painting have usually been those who were also the most prolific?)

All this is not to suggest that you divorce your wife and marry a brief case. It is simply meant to point up something so many copy people already practice—the profitability of sometimes adding to the regular hours of 9 to 5 a few of those after hours between 5 and 9.

CHAPTER 8

HOW TO SIZE AN ADVERTISEMENT

Should your advertisement occupy full-page space—or half page, quarter page, or even smaller? Some of the strategic, competitive, and other determining factors are discussed elsewhere in this book. But the subject itself deserves more complete discussion.

Basically, one of the best guides to a sound decision is this: What are you going to put into the advertisement? Many full pages contain sales angles which—because of their lack of breadth, depth, and intensity of appeal—don't really rate anything more than small space. On the other hand, some small-space advertisements present sales angles so strong in persuasion, and so universal in application, that they could profitably be "bumped up" into large space.

Your Vision May Be Too Narrow

Lack of imagination may even needlessly limit and circumscribe the scope and strength of a product's potential appeal. For example, one advertiser selling building materials used page space to sell the idea of "Building Your Own Darkroom in the Attic." That is probably overspacing, considering the limitations of that specific approach. At least it surely is, in comparison with the idea of "Building an Extra All-Purpose Room in the Attic," with attractive pictures and copy about the many uses of such a room. Conversely, another advertiser fully justifies his use of large space by broadening his market for office furniture. Instead of merely offering it as *merchandise,* he presents this powerful idea for purchasing it:

155

Now That Your Company Is Successful . . .
Does Your Office Look as
Though You're Still Struggling?

When you first started in business, your only interest was in keeping that business alive. You couldn't think how the office looked . . . so you grabbed a chair here, a table from there, even banged together your own cabinets and shelving.

Now that the success you fought for is yours, does your office look as though you're still struggling? Remember, one trick to holding on to success is to look like one.

Notice how this advertiser has tied his product up with a basic human appeal; how he has broadened his market beyond the relatively few people among the circulation of a publication who may have already come to the conclusion "on their own" that they may need new office furniture; how he has broken away from the common astigmatic fault of confining his approach to what his product *is*, rather than what it *does*. This kind of thinking creates advertising which richly rewards the use of larger space than might otherwise be justified.

Look Beyond the "Nuts and Bolts"

Countless advertisers are hidebound in their narrow conception of the function of their product. It is, they say, manufactured primarily for "this" purpose. So they never look imaginatively beyond the "nuts and bolts" of it. And they either use advertising space limited in size for reaching that particular market only—or, more commonly, they use space of a size which represents serious overspacing because their advertising approach is not as broadly based as it could be. Consequently, many smaller-space advertisers are underspacing, cutting down their sales volume because of preconceived fixations about the functions of their product. Likewise, many larger-space advertisers are overspacing because they do not really need such large space to present their own concept of the utility of a product

—even though it may actually possess the potentiality of mass-market sales.

Now, what can help you to decide which size space will do the best job for you? Well, compare these two space-buying procedures. One is to buy the space first and then decide what to put into it. The other (briefly mentioned in a preceding chapter) is the method often followed by advertisers who make every effort to check the results of their advertising. They do these four things:

1. Decide how far along the road to a completed sale they want that particular advertisement to propel the reader.

2. Determine which sales angles should be played up (and at what length) in order to stand the best chance of accomplishing that purpose.

Their decision as to this is based upon whatever figures or data they have, or can get, as to the demonstrated effectiveness of sales angles featured in previous advertisements or campaigns.

(Such case-history experience can be continually augmented by personal contacts, review of correspondence with consumers, consumer-research reports, dealer surveys, retail sales-clerk check-ups, etc.)

3. Then, after considering these factors, they decide what size space unit will be needed to display properly and to develop adequately their most effective sales angles.

4. And, finally, they buy space in that size unit.

If You Are Testing a New Product

Generally speaking, if you are testing a new product—or a new approach on an old product—it is wiser purposely to overspace, at least on your test advertising. This will enable you to present adequately and well what you feel are your most effective selling angles. On the other hand, if you underspace and the tests are not successful, you will always regretfully wonder whether you used space enough to do full justice to the proposition.

Here is a good line of reasoning. Larger space will permit you to do better justice to the copy appeal—and it may uncover a much broader market for the product than you ever imagined existed.

If the test ads flop, you at least can't reproach yourself with the fact that the failure might be entirely due to an incomplete presentation of sales angles. But if the tests are successful then you know that you are on the trail of a large-space, bigger-volume proposition. And even if the results of the tests are just on the fence, you can *then* experiment with tightening the copy up—and perhaps put it over the profit line by the use of a smaller unit of space. Furthermore, the use of larger space for your all-important test ads rates the very vital advantage of better position in the publication.

In conclusion, if you are going to put only one foot forward, make sure it is your best one. Because if *that* step doesn't get you anywhere, there isn't going to be any other one. If a proposition is worth testing at all, it's worth a good test.

And what can an advertiser lose on the cost of a test that really uses enough space to do a good job, copywise—as compared with what he can gain if the ad uncovers a new and profitable enterprise for him?

QUIZ ON CHAPTER 8

1. What is one good guide to a sound decision concerning the size to make your advertisement?

2. What mistake causes some advertisers to overspace?

3. What one causes others to underspace?

4. Of the two space-buying procedures cited, which is the sounder?

5. When is it wiser to purposely overspace?

SUBCUTANEOUS ADVERTISING

A rule-of-writing among newspaper reporters is "Start where the reader is." A suggestion which advertising copywriters may often use effectively is "Start where the reader *was.*" For most good advertisements, somehow and in some way, "get under the skin" of their readers—and one way to write a subcutaneous advertisement is to evoke a flood of nostalgic memories.

Sometimes you can do it positively, by making a comparison or tie-up with a *desirable* memory. Sometimes you can do it negatively, contrasting a new product advantage with an *undesirable* memory. Whether you use the positive or the negative, you've got the past experience of the five senses to hark back to.

With the sense of hearing, for example: a Victor Red Seal Record advertisement shows people applauding happily at the opera. The headline, "Call Back These Great Moments!" And Decca is selling albums of records of popular music of years gone by. The copy: "This music brings back golden memories. The tune you crooned in your heart . . . when you discovered you were in love! The melody you hummed on your honeymoon. The wonderful songs that old gang of yours harmonized . . . to the accompaniment of a beat-up ukulele . . . or around the family piano."

And when you are referring to seeing, tasting, smelling, or touching, you will be able to recall a host of other nostalgic images or pleasant experiences universally common to childhood, to youth, or to older times.

The use of such associations is particularly telling when you are advertising a new product which eliminates certain disadvantages that people have heretofore had to tolerate. Then you can commiserate with them awhile at the Wailing Wall before you exultingly invite them to raise their sorrowing eyes and walk hand in hand with you toward the Bright New Future.

So don't sell the old family album short. Getting out the memory book is one way of getting out a subcutaneous advertisement.

CHAPTER 9

DO COPY APPEALS HAVE A SEX?

First let me say that I am not a professional psychologist; nor is this chapter the result of any prior consultation with, or verification by, any authority in that field. It simply outlines some personal reflections and beliefs upon a subject which rightfully comes within the concern of the copywriter. I think that the opinions expressed are valid; your own experience may dictate otherwise.

There will probably be no disagreement with the statement that it is harder to sell things to women than to men—even basic commodities. The reasons for this are obvious. Here are two of them:

1. Women are the more careful buyers. Scrutinize values; compare prices, merchandise facts, ingredients; want pertinent particulars, and more of them. Men are inclined to "want what they want when they want it"; see it; buy it.

2. Women, on the more expensive items, don't usually have the "whole say" (or at least like to make us think they don't). Thus, instead of an individual decision on such items, a family pro-and-con discussion is involved—with the risk of inaction engendered by a delayed decision.

What do the basic psychological differences between men and women mean to the copywriter? Should they influence the kind of copy written? In what ways? First, what would be the general nature of these differences?

160

"Longer-Haul" Thinking

The man's general processes of thinking would, in the main, seem characterized by what might be called "longer-haul" thinking. The flow of his life and thoughts would perhaps represent more of a sweep, more of a tide. I am doubtless not expressing it well; but I mean that, both as a single and as a married man, his thoughts and concerns are, in a broad sense, associated with the future of himself and his family.

His thinking trend flows more naturally toward long-run things—his job, his rate of advancement, the ultimate educational advantages for his children, life insurance, security in later years, the future prospects of his company and of his position in it, etc. Of course, he has his daily concerns too; but, in its larger aspects, the man is more the guardian of the future. He is therefore more interested in, and cognizant of, the longer-haul influences and decisions that affect and determine it.

"Shorter-Haul" Thinking

On the other hand, it is not any derogation but merely an acceptance of the normal course of things to consider that women's processes of thinking are likely to be more "shorter-haul" in general character. Their lives are more sharply punctuated by separate events, the imminence of them and the immediate effects of them—circumstances concerned with dates, courtship, marriage, motherhood, daily problems of the children, the relation of specific events to social standing, the social significance of acquisitions, etc.

Of course, women are likewise concerned with problems of the future, just as men are concerned with problems of the present. But, again in its broader aspects, it is natural that their thinking trend should flow more strongly toward the more immediate, the more specific, and the shorter-haul causes and effects of things.

There is no need to go into a more detailed itemization of the predominating interests of each sex. But if you think about it for a moment you may agree, at least in a general way, with the contrast and differentiation mentioned above. To summarize: a man's life might perhaps be symbolized more as a tide, a woman's more as a succession of waves.

Do Your Observations Check with This One?

Since I am merely an amateur garden variety of psychologist, I do not know whether this underlying difference in thinking trends *is* a scientific fact. But I really think that it must be. Because it does seem to me that, in actual practice, the advertising which has already proven most notably effective in selling to women is that which is fully based, or which places most of its emphasis, upon the immediate, the imminent, or the specific. Think over the most successful campaigns addressed to women which you can recall, and see whether you do not come up with the same answer.

You will probably recollect quite a few examples which are broader in nature and general application. But I will contribute one which, although it occurred quite a few years ago, is still so noteworthy and memorable that you yourself probably still use a few of its headlines in your everyday language. It was the sensationally successful campaign which the then copywriter Lillian Eichler Watson wrote to sell *The Book of Etiquette,* which she herself had written.

Note the specificity, the tie-up with an immediate, imminent, expected, or desired event in these headlines:

> Again She Orders—"A Chicken Salad, Please"
> What's Wrong in This Picture?
> Why I Cried After the Ceremony
> May She Invite Him into the House?
> Suppose This Happened on Your Wedding Day

Of course, as I have said, each sex naturally does have its daily concerns: women likewise think long-haul thoughts, just as men think short-haul ones. But, in its larger aspects, a difference in thinking trends can condition the way each sex looks at, and reacts to, the appeals made in your advertising—and can even actually determine, in large measure, the degree and amount of response you get from it.

Why It Has Bearing on Your Copy

Therefore, if women's thinking trends are truly shorter-haul in character, then that fact must have a significant bearing upon how you may best address your advertising appeals to that sex. It seems wise to make doubly sure that your appeal be tied up with the immediate or the imminent; that it emphasize the specific and the right specific; and that, paradoxically, this specific nevertheless be general enough, in interest and application, to influence the largest possible number of your women readers.

Do the above observations seem valid to you? Are they borne out by your own observation or by your analysis of certain successful campaigns addressed to women? If so, this chapter then merely provides *post factum* confirmation of the lessons of experience. But even as such it may, by trying to trace effects back to their causes, serve to isolate and pin down a major reason for already-proven past effectiveness. And, by so doing, it may be used, *consciously,* as a guide to the preparation of more resultful copy addressed to women.

QUIZ ON CHAPTER 9

1. Why is it harder to sell to women?

2. What is meant by longer-haul thinking?

3. By shorter-haul thinking?

4. Cite two of the five shorter-haul headlines given.

5. What bearing does the difference in thinking patterns have upon the copy you write?

MR. JOHN JACQUES JONATHAN JONES

I have been reading the ads and articles in the trade papers. It looks to me as though it won't be so terribly long before American advertising starts doing a lot of foreign traveling. Therefore, I think it pertinent to relate this experience of an advertising man whom I know very intimately.

Some years ago this fellow was with a New York firm which had done a very successful job selling its product. The firm sent him to London to supervise the advertising program planned for the English market. He was also to go to Paris to do promotional work on it there.

He took with him proofs of the American advertising copy that had done a remarkably fine job here. Upon his arrival in London he showed these proofs to the various executives of his firm's British advertising agency. "Not the kind of advertising for *this* market at all," they said.

So this friend of mine talked the whole thing over with the general manager (as is usually the case, a Scotsman) of his firm's London branch. "Have them get up their own stuff entirely, then see how it looks to you," he was advised.

He did; the agency did; and he didn't like what *they* did. It just didn't seem to have the stuff he thought had made the American advertising so successful. Not that he blamed the agency. The proposition was completely new to them; whereas the American agency was thoroughly familiar with it and the copy had come out of a period of development. He realized that if a Britisher had come over to the States with the same problem, any American advertising man would be inclined to look at it the same way.

But—what to do? His New York office had given him his head, at least as far as the advertising itself was concerned. He wanted to make good.

Now this fellow was not any brilliant, knock-'em-dead ad man, as he himself would have been the first to admit. He even had a sneaking feeling that his firm had taken a long chance in sending him on this job. But everyone else was immersed in the big American operation, so the British experiment was looked upon as something of a side show.

Admitting he was no advertising ball-of-fire, he did get around to wondering whether, as far as truly basic sales appeals were concerned, the English John and the French Jacques were really so very different from the American Jonathan. And, as he said himself, he began to doubt whether Giovanni and Juan were so much different either.

Of course, market conditions, habits and almost everything else were utterly different. But he was thinking about basic human appeals and motivations—what Kipling was talking about, in a social sense, when he wrote that "the colonel's lady and Judy O'Grady are sisters under the skin." It was sure that this American advertising copy *did* get under the skin. There was no guesswork about the way it sent Americans into the department stores for the product. Why shouldn't it send English people into their "drapers," French people into the Galleries Lafayette and other stores?

So, scared stiff, he finally took his batch of ads over to the offices of the agency. "Take all of the Americanisms out of the copy," he told them. "But don't make any other changes in the copy or layouts. Then we'll start and see what happens."

To this day he doesn't know how much better, or poorer, the other copy might possibly have done. But the records show that his firm spent $60,000 for advertising in the year after the campaign started and that the receipts were $498,000.

This experience isn't a bad one to keep in mind, considering what's now on the horizon. Naturally, and rightly, we Americans are awed when we face the great differences in foreign markets. But remember, ads talk to *people.* And copy that works out fine here must have *something* in it that goes beneath mere nationality. Seems like the Johns, Jacques, Giovannis, Juans, Jonathans, *et al.* are all simply Joneses underneath—and if your copy has really got below American epidermis it's a valuable export.

P.S. I know that the above is true.
(I am the guy it happened to.)

CHAPTER 10

FACTS OR FANCIES—WHICH SHALL YOU FEATURE?

When I was nineteen I answered a Help Wanted ad in *Printers' Ink* for a cub copywriter. I still have the ad. Here is how it reads:

Cub Wanted

Successful New York agency offers a big chance for a young chap, just out of college, who loves books and wants to learn how to write about them. He must have imagination and something of the divine fire. Favorable symptoms would be a dabbling in verse and fiction. Yet we don't want any erotic neurasthenics with long hair. It's a man's job. Some literary ability, plus inspiration, plus hard common sense is about the prescription. If you think you can qualify and if you can begin at the bottom, tell the whole story in your first letter. "C.W.," Box 326, Care of *Printers' Ink*.

I almost got that job. I was the runner-up. And I've always wished I had started my advertising career with that as my first job. I would have been under the tutelage of Helen Woodward. So it would have been instructive and fascinating, I am sure. For Mrs. Woodward was the copywriter of some fabulous ads which were then making the whole country more familiar with the works of Mark Twain, O. Henry, and other authors. She was selling subscription sets for Harper & Brothers and other book publishers—and selling them like mad.

166

And no wonder. For her ads were delightful to read and irresistibly appealing. They made Huck Finn and Tom Sawyer come alive as vividly in the advertising pages of the many publications in which they appeared as their creator had done within the covers of his books. One of them became famous at the time. The copy was about Mark Twain himself, with the headline "He Walked with Kings." Then it continued:

> He could not know, standing there in his bare feet and his rough clothes, with his little schooling, that kings would do him honor when he died, and that all men who read would mourn a friend.
>
> He could not dream that one day his work would stand in Chinese, in Russian, in Hebrew, in Hungarian, in Polish, in French, in many languages he could not read—and from humble doorman to proudest emperor, all would be gladdened at his coming.
>
> He could not know that through it all he would remain as simple, as democratic, as he was that day as a boy on the Mississippi.

Later Mrs. Woodward wrote an autobiography, *Through Many Windows*. And one quotation from that book brings us to the subject of this chapter: "In writing good advertising it is necessary to put a mood into words and to transfer that mood to the reader. . . . I used to say to my copywriters when they were writing about books: Don't ever go to see the home of the author. Don't ever see the author himself. . . . Because, you see, when you know the truth about anything, the real, inner truth—it is very hard to write the surface fluff which sells it."

"The Most Wanted Product in the World"

Now, as other passages in Mrs. Woodward's book make fully clear (and as her own advertisements exemplified so brilliantly) what she meant by "surface fluff" is, I think, really the same thing that no less a realist than Jim Young meant when he wrote: "It is not sufficiently recognized—especially by the critics of advertising— that romance in its broad sense is the most wanted product in the world."

Some products are literally bursting with romantic and emotional connotations. Then it is wiser to stress the glamorous ideas associated with them—to feature the fancies and subordinate the facts, using the latter only to buttress the copy when and if necessary. With such products, copy too studded with "factory facts" can clip the wings of the reader's imagination. For example, the ad "Often a Bridesmaid, Never a Bride" wasn't loaded with prosaic facts about the ingredients in the product advertised. But it *was* loaded with "such stuff as dreams are made on."

Some Ads Don't Need Much Factual Underpinning

In other words, as with the Mark Twain ad, the copy about some products can soar successfully—without "coming a cropper." An abundance of factual material merely inhibits its flight. If too explicit about the "whys" and "hows," such copy pulls the reader's aroused imagination up short. Our much-quoted friend Napoleon touched on what I mean when he said, "The title of emperor is greater than that of king. Its significance is not wholly explicable, and therefore it stimulates the imagination."

The point was once brought out well in an article by Henry Huff. First, in a general reference, he writes:

> The job of the salesman and the advertising man, alike, is to lift his product out of the doldrums of the commonplace and into the realms of the dream world. We do not sell houses; we sell homes. We do not sell shoes; we sell foot comfort. We do not sell cosmetics, but sell the beauty that cosmetics enhance.

Then he gives a specific instance:

> A farmer and his wife decided that they had earned a rest; so they sold their little farm and moved to the neighboring village. After a few months, their first love returned and together they cast longing eyes upon the "Farms For Sale" ads in the village weekly. One day they read an ad that described a veritable "dream farm." It had everything that their imagination could contemplate.

They visited the local real estate man and a short time later were on their way to inspect the farm. Familiar roads were traversed, but it was not until the car had stopped that they discovered the advertised farm was the one they had once possessed. The "showmanship" ad had emphasized attractive features which they had not fully realized before!

Suppose the ad had confined itself solely to mundane "nuts and bolts" information about the number of rooms, plumbing, acreage, etc. Their interest would have dropped with a thud. Instead, it opened up a whole new world of romance and fascination.

So which shall you feature—facts or fancies? Of course, as with everything else, it depends upon the product or service; that determines the whether or not, or to what extent. If you are doing a hard-sell copy job that needs facts to support your claims, if it is obvious to you that your sales argument will topple over like a house of cards unless you support it with an underpinning of facts, read Chapter 3 again for suggestions. On the other hand, if you are sure you have, as Mrs. Woodward did, a product with a powerfully romantic, imaginative, and enchanting idea behind it, then do as John Keats suggested. "O sweet Fancy! let her loose."

QUIZ ON CHAPTER 10

1. What was called "the most wanted product in the world"?

2. When is it wiser to "feature the fancies and subordinate the facts"?

3. What was the headline of an ad about a well-known antiseptic which did this?

4. Why do some ads not need much "factual underpinning"?

5. What happens when you introduce this element into them?

ARE YOU AN "ADSOMNIAC"?

Perhaps, like many another copywriter, you know the mental meandering that follows the sudden awakening from a fitful sleep. And since, asleep or awake, most copywriters' minds swirl around with possible headlines and copy ideas, you might as well get up and jot them down. You'll lose them forever if you don't; you'll never go back to sleep unless you do.

Of course, even to the "adsomniac" himself, most of these ideas will sound terrible in the cold gray dawn. But, good or bad, you've got 'em—and they won't bother you any more. Some you may even use. Perhaps, for example, just before you went to sleep you purposely put what Bob Updegraff called "your subconscious fireless-cooker" to work on a particularly tough copy problem. It sometimes happens (for me, at least) that the cooker door pops open with the perfect headline or copy slant. Who cares then what time A.M. it is! (Except, of course, one's also-awakened wife.)

Now, as long as we are taking our crew cuts down together, let's put our Marcel Proust or Virginia Woolf outfits on and see what kind of stuff floats down this "stream of consciousness." Here are some examples, none of which will be of the slightest use to you:

Say, I got that same letter again from an insurance company. I get it several times a year. I've heard it's very successful. It contains only 49 words! These ask you firmly but politely to furnish your date of birth—so that the company can send you some information about a certain policy.

Did you ever hear of such a way to get action? By effrontery, no less. It's brash, superconfident. There's a kind of compulsion, an hypnotic mesmerism about it. I guess the people who respond are induced by the asker's obvious expectancy and certainty. I wonder what account we could use *that* kind of selling for?

Say, I've been 40 years in a copy department! No, come to think of it, that anniversary will come *next* November. After all those years, I sure ought to know something to do with the slant that taxi driver gave me yesterday. He told me women practically never have their fares ready. That they don't even start to fumble around in their cluttered bags for it until after they reach their destination. But most men glance at the meter a block or so in advance, figure out the tip, and hand the money to the cabbie as they get out. It's not that a man's pocket is so much easier to get something out of. Cabbies say it's a different kind of mind. I wonder what psychologists say about this . . . and what, if anything, could be done about it, copywise?

Say, what about that guy who told me the shower head in his shower had not worked properly for years? And when I asked him why he didn't have it fixed or get a new one, he said it never gave him *enough* trouble for that! I guess most people never do anything to correct an annoyance or difficulty unless it becomes a *real* pain in the neck. There's certainly a copy angle there that I can use some-time. Get up and write it down, you dope!

Say, that was a good article I read about "The Deadliest Error of Our Time." One single wrongly used word caused the atom bomb to be dropped on Japan—and enabled the Russians to cash in big by declaring war on Japan just before the war ended. Japan's message to the U.S.A. said that she was "ignoring" the peace terms offered. But they had used a word which, translated, also meant "withholds comment" upon the terms which were extended. Boy, can one word louse up the resultfulness of an ad too! Remember that time, in an ad addressed to women, I had something in it about "snakes." Even used a *picture* of one. Phew, I prefer to forget the number of replies it pulled, or rather, didn't!

Say, what about that famous restaurant and night club I pass on the way to work every morning? Best-known one in America, I guess. At that time, a truck is always there delivering crates of ginger ale. And do those dingy bottles look unglamorous and unappetizing. Not worth a nickel. Yet that same night—in the club's opulent, glistening surroundings—each bottle will look almost worth the dollar they charge for it. There certainly is a copy and art idea there. Got to remember that.

Say, I must do some more of what I did the other day. With a full-page ad to write, I decided to write it first as if it were to be a very small one. Guess that's a good way to make you concentrate on the truly biggest selling points, to cut out all the little cluttery claims. It sifts out the men from the boys—and the final longer copy was a lot stronger.

Say, that ad about the motion picture *Titanic* was a peach. I heard that the man who wrote the book was an ad man. Maybe he wrote the copy. It said something about: "One instant their intimate drama raged . . . and the next they were all engulfed in the greatest human story ever told!" Let's see, what did I want to remember about that? Oh yes, that and some of the other copy got the *personal* into it, made it clear that this movie was really a personal story about the emotions of people, not an impersonal documentary portraying an event alone. As Rudolf Flesch says, "Get *people* into your copy."

Naturally, if you too suffer from "adsomnia," we both could go on and on with this article. But why? If other people don't realize by now that this malady can help you more than it can hurt, then more wordage about it won't get us anywhere anyway, will it?

CHAPTER 11

FOURTEEN INTERESTING AND INSTRUCTIVE SPLIT-RUN TESTS

I once heard a talk in which the speaker listed twenty possible variables that can occur in the "test town" copy-testing programs most commonly used. These, as you probably know, are programs in which various towns or cities are selected for the testing of different types of advertising on the same product. The comparative sales results of the different appeals used in the advertising are determined by a check-up of the quantity of the product which has been sold, based on a shelf count of the stock in the dealers' stores before and after the advertising has appeared.

The "twenty possible variants" referred to in the above-mentioned talk made the good clean split-run test of "Ad A vs. Ad B" sound pretty much like the answer to the ad man's prayer.

Sufficiently Conclusive—if Properly Handled

Of course, split runs are perhaps not the ultimate in copy-testing techniques. But, amidst the hazy atmosphere surrounding various factors in some of the other methods, split runs do shine through with an awfully nice white light of comparative finality.

For—instead of requiring the adjusting, discounting, and compensating for this, that, and the other variable—Ad A and Ad B each run in the same publication; in the same position and size of space; on the

173

same insertion date. Each goes to half the circulation and is distributed equally, geographically and numerically, on the stands or by mail or carrier. Each ad carries a coupon with a different key number, so that the comparative results can be accurately measured.

The split-run tests I am going to tell you about were made in publications with large circulations. The space used was also large, mainly full pages. These two factors provided a sufficient quantity of comparative response to be accurately indicative. The differences in America's social and economic scale were well represented by these publications. And the figures were not tabulated until the lapse of a period adequate for all but the straggling response which would not change the accuracy of the picture—not less in any case than three months after publication.

Differences Should "Scream"—not "Whisper"

No split runs are included here in which the difference in result between Ad A and Ad B was not *greater* than 15 per cent. Why? Because those advertising men who are most familiar with split-run techniques don't have much faith in "figures that whisper"; unless the figures "scream" they don't hear them very well.

Such men even make split-run tests of split runs—by occasionally taking the very same ad, without the slightest change of any kind *except* for key number, and running it A and B against itself.

If the disparity in the comparative result of that incestuous experiment is too great, they run like mad to the publication and demand a check-up on the physical division and distribution of that issue.

But what do they consider "too great"? Not fractions, nor a few measly percentage points! "Too great" means ABOVE 15 per cent—because they have discovered that even split runs which they have had checked back for accuracy can vary that much *on the very same ad*. Why, no one knows—but there it is! So that is why the split-run examples referred to here contain no difference of less than 15 per cent in result.

The General Application of Split-Run Experience

In the following examples I have first discussed mail-order conclusions. Then, secondly, I discuss general applications—because I believe that there will be sufficient useful information and analogies here for the *non*mail-order man to draw his own, and perhaps much wider, parallels.

A WELL-KNOWN COMPANY VS. AN UNKNOWN ONE:

Test: Advertisement signed with a well-known company name pulled 28.2 per cent better than the same advertisement signed with an unknown one.

Mail-Order Conclusion: The wonder here is that the "unknown name" advertisement did as well as it did, comparatively. For one company name was "manufactured" simply for this test; nobody had ever heard of it. Whereas the known name was one of the most famous in its field, which is a very large consumer-product one. Furthermore, the product advertised was one concerned with the reader's health—a subject in which the reader's confidence in a company name well and favorably known to the public should have represented a really tremendous "plus."

The experience of mail-order men, however, is that the reader is primarily interested in what a product will *do* for him. *Who* makes it is, of course, good substantiation for the claims made and is very important as proof material; nevertheless, many products which have a wide sale and which do a good job for the consumer are sold by firms whose names are not of great sales value in themselves.

General Application: Logotypes given top-of-ad or center display might well be relegated to minor "downstairs" position in many advertisements—and the top prominence be given to the story of what the product will do for the reader. The inordinately conspicuous display of the advertiser's name assures the readership of the advertiser himself . . . but not necessarily that of the readers of the publication.

SHOULD AN OFFER BE "BURIED" OR DISPLAYED?

Test No. 1: Advertisement with offer displayed conspicuously did 52.9 per cent better.
Test No. 2: 68 per cent better.
Test No. 3: 110.3 per cent better
Test No. 4: 20.8 per cent better
Test No. 5: 28.7 per cent poorer
Test No. 6: 29.4 per cent poorer

Mail-Order Conclusion: Good practice in the mail-order field generally indicates the advisability of playing up an obviously attractive offer prominently, rather than consigning it to a minor position in the advertisement. Sometimes it is worked into the headline itself, otherwise given conspicuous "upstairs" display.

In two of the instances cited above (where the top display of the offer did poorer), the advertisement which did better was an exceptionally fine and intriguing piece of narrative copy, but with the offer strongly featured at the *bottom* of the ad.

However, as mail-order men know from bitter experience, "exceptionally fine" copy is *sui generis;* it is safer to bet that, on the average, most copy will not rate any higher encomium than "good."

General Application: Many general (*non*-mail-order) advertisers run "buried-offer" test advertisements in such small space, in such light schedules, and in publications of such small or unrepresentative circulations that the final results prove nothing—with each ad pulling just a few more or less inquiries than others in the test campaign. Such tests are valueless. Yet some advertisers—based upon this inadequate evidence—go on to shoot the works nationally, gambling, without realizing it, upon a copy appeal which has not really proven itself!

Even variations in the position of the different ads can account *entirely* for the difference in result, without any true indication whatever of the comparative strength of the appeals being tested.

To eliminate this: use a large enough schedule, in a publication with a sizable circulation, or a group of smaller ones for verification—

so that you get sufficient inquiries to *prove* something. Or use larger ads, so that position variations average more fairly. Or combine the same offer *and* the various appeals being tested into the headlines or top display—thus getting a greater quantity of inquiries and also a test of copy appeals at the same time.

OF HOW MUCH VALUE IS COLOR IN A PRODUCT?

Test No. 1: 182 per cent more inquiries for a product obtainable in color as against black-and-white
Test No. 2: 83 per cent more inquiries
Test No. 3: 224 per cent more inquiries
Test No. 4: 26 per cent more inquiries

Mail-Order Observation: The product in each case was an article of home decoration. In each advertisement the price was clearly stated. The increased results quoted about were obtained despite the fact that the color price was 50 per cent more than the black-and-white price.

General Application: The sales attractiveness of many products could doubtless be greatly enhanced by the addition of color—even in the case of various "hard goods" products, strictly utilitarian in purpose, in which at first thought color might not seem necessary or additionally appealing.

HOW STRONG IS THE APPEAL OF ATTRACTION TO THE OPPOSITE SEX?

Test No. 1: Article with this appeal did 211 per cent better than one concerned with the success-in-business appeal.
Test No. 2: Article with this appeal did 223.5 per cent better than one concerned with the selection of a vocation.

Mail-Order Conclusion: If a proposition has in it a legitimate appeal based upon one's popularity with, or attractiveness to, the other sex—

and if that appeal can be tied up *relevantly* with the product—use it.

General Application: This is, of course, already widely done in *non*mail-order advertising, but sometimes irrelevantly, absurdly, and merely to capture attention—and without any true tie-up with the product. However, many general advertisers who could use the appeal logically, legitimately, and inoffensively do not do so.

DO BUSY LAYOUTS ATTRACT—OR REPEL—ATTENTION?

Test No. 1: Advertisement with busy layout did 39 per cent better than layout that was more symmetrically balanced and artistically unified.

Test No. 2: 111.5 per cent better

Test No. 3: 30 per cent better

Mail-Order Conclusion: Mail-order men do not worry about layouts being too busy. They don't shy away from running ads that are spotty, with plenty of units strewn around all over the place—as long as the units are interesting and relevantly substantiate and advance the copy argument.

General Application: Page after page of beautifully balanced artistically correct layouts—obviously carefully prepared by professionals —certainly neutralize each other in the magazine, although they do look handsome on the drawing boards. They do not look like newsy messages coming direct (seemingly) from the advertiser to his readers. Instead, they are concoctions obviously painstakingly planned by his advertising people.

Is an advertisement an art gallery . . . or a market place? There's more *Stop!* if some busyness is added—and if people don't stop they can't shop.

SHOULD A "CHOICE" BE OFFERED?

Test No. 1: Advertisement featuring "choice of four" did 16.1 per cent better than ad offering but one "model"

Test No. 2: "Choice of three" did 19.7 per cent better

Test No. 3: "Choice of three" did 30.4 per cent better

Test No. 4: "Choice of six" did 52.6 per cent better than "choice of four"

Test No. 5: "Choice of six" did 94 per cent better than that featuring only one

Test No. 6: "Choice of six" did 261.8 per cent better than that featuring only one

Mail-Order Conclusion: "Which of these do you prefer?" is a sales pitch commonly used in mail-order selling—just as "Which of these models do you prefer?" is part of the closing talk often used by salesmen, even *before* the prospect has definitely decided to buy any model at all.

General Application: Privilege of choice can often broaden the potential. In any big block of publication circulation there are thousands to whom the inexpensive is costly, any ornamentation in design is gingerbread, the small is too large, the classical is "corny," the beautiful is ugly, the natural is artificial—*et al, ad infinitum,* and vice versa throughout the whole gamut. When space permits, many advertisers could sample their line more completely . . . hitting more targets by using a shotgun instead of a rifle.

DOES NOSTALGIA PAY?

Test: Advertisement which worked in considerable nostalgic copy and related pictures did 41 per cent better than one which used none of it at all.

General Application: The advertising appeal on lots of products ties in naturally and relevantly with pleasant nostalgic memories; and, when the product has corrective advantages or uses, unpleasant nostalgic recollections may be evoked in a human way. "Remember how you used to have to . . . but *now* . . ." Getting out the memory book is one way of getting out a subcutaneous ad.

HAS THE APPEAL BEEN UNNECESSARILY NARROWED?

Test: Advertisement based upon the appeal of the widest utility of the product pulled 100 per cent better than one based upon a specialized appeal.

Mail-Order Observation: In mail-order practice the usual objective is to find and to use effectively the widest possible appeal to an audience with selective interests. This is not a contradiction of terms. The purpose is to get *immediate* action from as many as possible of the people who are, or can be, interested in the advantages of owning what may be a specialized product.

Even though the market may be a selective one, the attempt is constantly made to find appeals which will get more orders *within* the market—and of course to broaden the size of the market, too. The test referred to above is the record of one such effort.

General Application: The *non*mail-order advertiser who sells products which have an appeal broader than the mail-order advertiser's often confines himself to appeals that are more narrow and selective than they need be. The product intrinsically (and its unexploited adaptabilities, inherently) may justifiably warrant different and wider selling appeals than are now being used.

In many cases the product's additional potential uses are not even smoked out, let alone exploited. The manufacturer makes it, advertises it, and sells it—using but one of its utilities as his selling appeal. There may be many others, perhaps stronger ones. Sometimes the public even writes enthusiastic letters telling him how they are using his own product for purposes he himself never dreamed of. Often "thar's gold in them files" . . . and in some product and consumer research.

HOW STRONG IS "NEWNESS" AS AN APPEAL?

Test No. 1: 75.4 per cent better
Test No. 2: 79 per cent better

Mail-Order Conclusion: If a product has a factor of newness in it mail-order men always feature that element strongly—using headlines which convey the assurance that a new product (or a new way, new discovery, new ingredient, new invention) will do something which people want done for them.

General Application: As discussed in Chapter 1 of this book, Americans do not suffer from neophobia. Things that are new or novel attract them. It is not safe to rely too abjectly upon the copy pitch about the old, dependable, "established in 1898" product. Today's public expects constant *improvement* in products—and if people don't get that assurance from a well-known firm, they will change loyalties to an even totally unknown one that announces it convincingly.

HOW MUCH SAFER IS IT TO OFFER A "SMALLER COMMITMENT"?

Sometimes a manufacturer tries to increase his sales unit by *requiring* the public to purchase more than one of an article. In some cases this can lead to a commitment which discourages sales.

Test No. 1: "Buy one" did 77.2 per cent better than "buy two"
Test No. 2: 111 per cent better
Test No. 3: 67.6 per cent better
Test No. 4: 47.4 per cent better
Test No. 5: "Buy two" did 68.6 per cent better than "buy five"
Test No. 6: "Buy a half dozen" did 22.9 per cent better than "buy a dozen"

Mail-Order Conclusion: General practice is to offer the number of units which figures show will produce the most profitable net, but always avoiding a commitment of a size which will discourage sales.

The increase of the commitment is usually made a *voluntary* act on the part of the purchaser. Since some people are naturally more fully sold by the advertising than others (or are already "more in the market" for it), mail-order men give those people a chance to "write their own ticket," to trade up beyond the minimum requirement.

General Application: Soft drink and electric bulb manufacturers, for example, offer multiple-unit packages. Such items are of course readily expendable. (And one may also buy single units if one prefers.) There is a danger, however—when the single-unit price of an article is small—in offering it *only* in multiple—unit packages for which the public sees no quick or necessary usability.

On the other hand, there are certainly many small-price products which could readily be sold in units of more than one, or which could be combined with other closely related (and equally necessitous) ones.

HOW GOOD IS A FREE-EXAMINATION OFFER

Test No. 1: 60.4 per cent better
Test No. 2: 97.6 per cent better
Test No. 3: 24.3 per cent better
Test No. 4: 35.2 per cent better

Mail-Order Conclusion: All of these experiments were based upon a five-day free-examination offer of the product, as compared with a full commitment to purchase, *without* free examination. Of course it was necessary to see how these trial customers "converted" into full-fledged ones. The ratio in all four cases was satisfactory.

General Application: Not commonly applicable outside the mail-order field. However, this offer can sometimes be made in co-operation with retailers. Also, this split-run experience indicates to general advertisers the advisability of at least using a strong money-back assurance whenever possible. And many general advertisers completely pass up this strong selling inducement!

HOW STRONGLY DO WOMEN REACT TO A LOWER PRICE?

Test No. 1 ($2.00 price vs. $2.50): $2.00 price was 62.2 per cent better

Test No. 2 ($2.75 price vs. $1.98): $1.98 price was 87 per cent better

Conclusion: In both tests the article sold was the same, and the ads were the same, except for the difference in prices. Of course, no one needed this test (involving 2,000,000 circulation) to prove what we all know about the purchasing habits of women. But the advertiser had a very tight margin for profit at a $2.00 selling price—and wanted desperately to find out if he could get a higher price for the article. He couldn't—and still get the volume of sales he needed.

"MERCHANDISING" MANY APPEALS OR SELECTING ONE TO FEATURE?

Test: "Merchandising many" 39 per cent better

Conclusion: If your experience makes you positive about the effectiveness of one appeal it is better to feature it. However, if you are not sure, it is better to "merchandise" the product thoroughly, specifying the various different appeals. Then the prospect can shop around in the ad for the advantages which hit him hardest.

PICTURING THE PRODUCT IN USE VS. SHOWING IT ONLY AS MERCHANDISE

Test: "Product in Use" 111.5 per cent better

Conclusion: Usually it's more persuasive to use pictures of the product in actual use rather than merely as an article of inert merchandise, and depending on words alone to describe the advantages of owning it.

QUIZ ON CHAPTER 11

1. Under what circumstances is a split-run test sufficiently conclusive?

2. Why are no examples given of differences in results representing less than 15 per cent?

3. Which dangers should you avoid when making a "buried-offer" test?

4. How much better were the results when the *newness* of the product was stressed?

5. How strongly did women react to a lower price in the two examples cited?

TO THE JONESES

(Concerning the much-lamented and often-publicized *"unfortunate sociological tendency, so typical of Americans: trying to 'keep up with the Joneses' "* . . .)

Neanderthal Jones just gave to *his* mate
  A brand-new fur of great attraction.
How long must I sit in this cave and wait?
    Go hit the trail . . . let's see some action!"
(Said Ann T. Diluvian to Stone Age Smith)

It gnaws at my bones when Jupiter Jones
Goes skimming by in his nifty chariot.
Let's buy a *new* model, encrusted with stones;
  I'll earn some more drachmas to carry it!"
(Said Socrates Smith to spouse, Xantippe)

"Now why do *we* have to spend all our life
  In a shack any bear could smash with his paw?
Did you see the new home Jones built for *his* wife?
  So, Pioneer Smith—go trot out your saw!"
(Said Samantha Smith to husband, Pioneer)

Oh, it's horrible, Americans,
　To exhibit such a stain.
Wanting things "beyond your sta-
　　tion"
　Makes you need a better train.

It's so nice and soft and easy
　For a vegetating gent
To coagulate with others
　In gelatinous Content!

"Man wants but *little* here below";
　(Could Goldsmith have been
　　wrong?)
For then he comes along and says:
　"Nor wants that little long."

But don't let ad men make you

Think 'way "above your place."
Their minds are fixed on "fifteen-
　　two,"
　And how to fill up space.

They'll make you think ambitious
　　thoughts
　About new things—you'll yearn
　　'em!
They'll force you to improve your-
　　self
　And rate the dough to earn 'em.

To "keep up with the Joneses,"
　　man,
　Is nothing to eschew,
If tied up with your larger plan
　To build a better you!

CHAPTER 12

"CUMULATIVE EFFECT"—A COMMON ALIBI FOR POOR ADVERTISING

The habit of waiting for, and placing great dependence upon, cumulative effect can become simply an alibi for poor advertising. It is like the story of the graying bachelor and the faded spinster, back in the old home town. Ed hoped Hattie would finally say yes. He had been asking her for years. He had implicit faith in the power of repetition and in eventual force of cumulative effect. But a new suitor could probably have swept Hattie right off her feet—with one really knockout of a sales talk which contained the very same fundamentals we have discussed in this book.

Of course, it is acknowledged that advertising has an accruing value. But the mistake is in trying to justify copy which isn't doing a demonstrably good job by saying, "Well, sales will *zoom* when we begin to feel the cumulative effect!"

Why Multiply Zero?

One of the investigations made by Dr. Henry C. Link indicated that an advertising theme that does not have a strong effect immediately is not likely to accumulate much in effectiveness through periodic repetition over a period of months. If an advertising campaign just doesn't click with sales when it is fresh and new, it is not wise (and it *is* costly) to keep betting for a long period on that particular copy approach. Mere dogged repetition of an appeal which hasn't given

186

any proof whatever of persuasive power is unlikely to cause sales to pyramid later. After all, zero multiplied by *any* number is still zero!

Even though cumulative effect is recognized as a valuable force in advertising, is is safer to look upon it as a bonus earned by advertising which is *proving* that it is doing a good selling job—but not as any justification for unsupported faith in the mere repetition of advertising which isn't.

When you leave out one or more of the basic fundamentals of a good advertisement, or when you use them poorly, you are writing advertising that is not as effective as it might be—or you are, consciously or unconsciously, depending on future advertisements or upon cumulative effect to do part of the job you yourself should be doing in each advertisement you write.

False Reliance upon the "Series" Idea

In explaining why one or more of the basic elements may be omitted from a given advertisement it is often claimed that these will be covered in later advertisements in the series. But it is much sounder to operate on the basis that each advertisement should be a complete and integrated selling presentation. Each advertisement has a job to do and should take the specific steps necessary to reach its goal.

So do not rely upon a whole series of advertisements to do a job which a single properly written advertisement can do. (People are not following your series with bated breath.) Do not depend upon cumulative effect to produce ultimately the action which a really good piece of copy, with all the basic fundamentals present and well employed, can accomplish at once.

What's Profitable about Procrastination?

The purpose of most advertisements is to sell goods. If three pieces of copy seem to be needed to persuade the individual prospect, then something was lacking in the first and second pieces. The goal of each separate advertisement should be to make the reader say yes—and act. The cash value of "maybe" or a "not now but later" is nil. Yet the very theory of cumulative effect is based upon the eventual value of such procrastination!

Let us further consider how much actual checkable value is inherent in the cumulative effect of advertising. There is no question but that trade names and copy themes which have been before the public for many years have great entrenched sales value. But the theory of cumulative effect itself has cost advertisers more lost time and money (and has glossed over more inefficient advertising) than perhaps any other single factor in the field of advertising.

Anyone who has worked with advertisers whose sales must come direct from their advertising knows that they cannot afford to wait for any pie-in-the-sky cumulative effect. To them the cumulative theory is too expensive an excuse for low initial sales, slow pick-up in volume, or poor pulling power. They know that each of their advertisements must prove that it can pay for itself. And by pay, they mean bring in enough actual, traceable dollars to cover the cost of space, the cost of the merchandise it sells, and then show a clear profit to the advertiser.

Now if blind faith in the force of cumulative effect were justified, the tenth advertisement using the same copy approach (each one of which has first been carefully tested for its own effectiveness) would produce more business than the first one. It does not—and the records of any advertiser who has been able to keep an ad-by-ad account of his operations will prove it.

Unfortunately, however, a new campaign is often released for publication with its component parts entirely untested. And when some signs of profitable response are noticed at about the time the sixth or seventh insertion appears, the credit is chalked up to cumulative effect. It does not always occur to the advertiser that the simple superiority of the sixth or seventh piece of copy alone may account for that sudden life.

What's the Cumulative Cost in Time and Money?

Cumulative proponents may assert that so-and-so's business, which started out with only a thousand or ten thousand sales a month and has multiplied that volume a dozenfold, is proof that accumulated advertising means accelerated sales. But how much has it taken? Too often many years—and many thousands, or even millions. Think how many advertisers, after having placed enough space to acquire a theoretical accumulation of customers to last until doomsday, have suddenly found that, to their consternation, the inspired copy approach of some new upstart his bitten into a huge section of their markets.

What must also be borne in mind is that the apparent cumulative effect of some campaigns lies not in any persuasiveness of the advertising itself. It can represent merely the number of repeat sales from customers already won, sales that have been mistakenly credited to the supposed cumulative effectiveness of the advertising.

You're Not in an Endurance Contest

So let us get rid of the expensive notion that cumulative effect is the greatest force in advertising. Good selling should not be an endurance contest between the advertiser and the consumer. To be worth its salt an advertisement should start at once to do a thorough selling job—from its headline to its closing bid for action—without taking for granted any of the effort that has gone before, and without leaving any part of the job unfinished for whatever effort may come after.

After that, whatever cumulative effect may accrue is well and good. Before that, any abject dependence upon cumulative effect can be merely an alibi for poor advertising. If not sufficiently supported by a preponderance of evidence of the selling ability of one's present advertising, sublime confidence in the future magic of cumulative effect reminds me of the story about the man who was buried in quicksand up to his neck. When asked if he wanted any help he replied cheerily, "No, I've got a good horse under me!"

QUIZ ON CHAPTER 12

1. What did the investigation made by Dr. Link indicate about "cumulative effect"?

2. What is the safer way to evaluate the influence of cumulative effect?

3. Why is it unwise to rely upon the "series" idea?

4. When does cumulative effect often mistakenly get credit for an improvement in the responsiveness of advertising?

5. Why can unsupported faith in cumulative effect be merely an alibi for poor advertising?

CHAPTER 13

THE HARD-BOILED ATTITUDE—AND HOW TO ACQUIRE IT

Although the subject of this book is not the writing of mail-order advertising, this type of experience nevertheless does build into the very core of a copywriter an attitude toward advertising which I believe every good copywriter must either already possess or, to remain good, must consciously acquire. And by "good copywriter" I mean one whose all-absorbing aspiration on every copy job is the production of sales, not the production of compliments. And that definition applies without regard to *what* the product is or *how* and *where* it is sold.

So that is why I am devoting this chapter to a full discussion of how *any* copywriter can achieve this aspiration more frequently— through the acquisition of what I call the "Hard-Boiled Attitude."

What's Behind *This Attitude?*

Now, what's behind this hard-boiled attitude? Why does it permeate the thinking of the experienced mail-order man? How does he acquire it? And how can a copywriter who is not in the field of mail order weave it into his creative fiber? In order to answer the latter question, let us first examine at some length why this attitude dominates the activities of the mail-order copywriter. That will also give us a clearer definition of what this hard-boiled attitude really is.

191

Years ago, one of the hits of the vaudeville stage was a comic named Will Mahoney. He was a dancer of tremendous vitality. He jigged and he danced until he was bathed in perspiration. He fell and he climbed, did splits and somersaults; wrestled with himself, climbed up the props. Finally, exhausted, he fell upon his stomach. Then, leaning on one elbow and facing the audience, he said in a plaintive voice: "There *must* be easier ways than this to make a living."

That same feeling often comes to advertising men who for years have successfully wrestled with the problem of making direct-result mail-order advertising pay its own way . . . and a profit besides.

Day after day, with the actual record cards in front of their clients, they must prove that they can write copy that really sells. They get no "yearly appropriations." If their keyed copy pays a profit, and if the record cards prove to their client that it does, they keep the account and get some more billing.

On the other hand, if their copy flops (and the record cards never hide that either), they don't keep their clients very long. For such clients are not the kind of advertisers who will accept alibis or keep barking up the wrong tree while they wait for the cumulative effect.

No plums of "easy billing" drop into the laps of advertising men whose clients live on coupons. The billing they get is determined by the results they produce. So it's no wonder that they, too, often feel that "There *must* be easier ways than *this* to make a living!"

But There Are Two Compensations

Of course, it isn't easy to make advertising pay a profit in direct, checkable results. It is a tough school of experience. But, like any other difficult type of work carried on successfully over the years, there is a big factor of compensation in it.

In fact, there are two such factors. And both are equally valuable to advertisers of all kinds—whether their copy carries coupons for direct results, or whether they have retail outlets. (Actually, getting customers into the stores—where they can see, hear, smell, touch, or even sample the taste of the product itself—is obviously easier than getting people to detach, sign, enclose, stamp, address, and mail an order for something merely described, sometimes by an advertiser entirely unknown to them.)

Here is the first factor. Advertising men who "get good marks" in this keyed-copy school of experience gain something they can never lose; something they could not buy; something that cannot be acquired on short order when the need for it suddenly arises; something which comes out of the years and becomes an ingrained part of them which they apply, consciously or instinctively, to every advertising problem they face throughout their entire business lives.

When Is an Ad "Good"?

This "something" is, in short, a certain *attitude* toward advertising itself: a hard-boiled, uncompromising, cost-plus way of looking at every single phase of any advertising job, from the smallest to the largest. Every agate line of space costs money; what goes into each one must contribute its bit toward a profit. And the completed advertisement is not "good" because its writer likes it, or because the client, his wife, or his friends "think" it is good. The purpose of an advertisement is to produce a profit—and it is demonstrably good only if and when it proves that it can do so.

This constant, unwavering focus on What Are the Actual Sales and What Is It Costing to Produce Them? makes tough demands on advertising which only good copy can fulfill. But unless such demands *are* made upon it, advertising can become soft and ineffectual—as is so evident in every publication you pick up.

That describes the Hard-Boiled Attitude. Briefly, it represents the difference between the soft, based-on-hope attitude of Micawber, who, if he had written an ad, would have hoped "something would turn up" as a result of it—and the hard, based-on-experience attitude of Thomas A. Edison, who, after experimenting with different ideas for almost ten years, could only reply to a friend who had asked him what he had learned that he had in his pocket a notebook listing three thousand things that he positively knew would *not work*.

Knowing and Avoiding That Which Is Most Likely to Fail

That anecdote about Edison brings us to the second factor of compensation acquired by advertising men who must make their copy prove, by sales figures, that it is producing a profit for their clients.

Of course, years of experience in writing, testing, and checking the results of couponed advertisements naturally lead to some dependable opinions as to what has the best chance of paying out; what copy appeals; which types of headline or layout.

But, in addition to such knowledge of a positive nature, this experience also builds a valuable fund of what might be called "negative knowledge." By this I mean the ability to know and to avoid that which has proved unsuccessful so frequently in the past that it is all too likely to fail if tried again. For it is not only important to know what to do but also (as Edison's notebook warned) what not to do: to know the location of the red lights of danger and loss as well as the green lights of safety and gain.

In other words, since every proposition has basic differences in it, even the mail-order man does not learn with certainty the ideas which are bound to succeed in all circumstances. But he does learn a number of things which just will not work. He learns many things to avoid, many mistakes or pitfalls to sidestep, certain things which are so very wrong to do that a fatal resultlessness will unquestionably follow if he does them.

More Nays than Yeas

In fact, over the years it does seem that the mail-order man acquires a bigger arsenal of noes than of yeses. The yeses may apply on one proposition but not on another; but the noes seem to have a way of being more applicable to any proposition. Perhaps (as in life itself) what is right to do is more likely to be more *specifically* right—but what is wrong is more likely to apply *generally*.

As an example of this, I have found (despite my long experience in the field) that it is not too hard to weed out those ads which I am pretty sure are the very poorest among a group; but I frankly cannot with much accuracy select those which are "bound to succeed." (Badness in everything is so much more obvious and dramatic than goodness, isn't it?)

Thus, it follows that another trait which the mail-order man soon learns (or should learn) is humility. It has been said that people with little ability are inclined to overrate themselves; those with great ability to underrate themselves. Ralph Starr Butler puts it this way:

> "I have known, perhaps, more people in advertising than most—the truly great, the transitory great, the near-great, the show-offs, the stupids, the struggling youngsters on the way up, the tired men who "arrived" and didn't know what to do about it—and the few who did. . . . But all the truly great, according to my private definitions, have in common one quality: they have humility.

The Tougher the Job, the Better the Copy

Now, because the mail-order man sells goods the hard way, he must scratch for business. This toughness builds up the habit of tearing the product apart and finding every possible use and sales appeal for it. He (like any good copywriter, regardless of the type of copy he writes) does not merely look upon a piece of merchandise and dilate about its intrinsic external or internal specifications. He sees it *in use*—not merely as a physical product but as a servant.

This makes him look, in surprise and sometimes with derision, at much of the advertising he reads. He immediately sees many selling opportunities either muffed entirely or given inadequate treatment—or even totally eliminated. He reads ads on products which fairly burst with good selling angles, usabilities, advantages, and appeals. Yet because the copy did not come from a typewriter battered with bucking hard selling jobs, it may be based on a purely merchandise presentation or may be so pallid that the sales points are virtually washed out.

Clyde Bedell, in his book *How to Write Advertising That Sells,* puts it this way:

Pick up any fat newspaper or magazine. For every ad you find which dramatizes some important and fundamental point, or series of points, you will find at least one ad which in a gentle ladylike way marches from the first word to the last in modified goose step.

The ads that have wallop at strategic places are likely to be the ads of people who have built their successes on selling or on selling by mail. They are likely to be the advertisers who have made consumer demand for their products their fetish.

The ads that are gentle and without guile are the ads of people who have never had to rely on advertising to get out in the brash market and bite and kick their way to success. They have depended more on salesmen or on dealers whom they could induce to sell their lines.

Nowadays, competition for many products is savage and aggressive. Some advertisers view the competition they have in publications and on the air and make up their minds their advertising has to put on overalls and go to work. When that happens, they begin to check and test. They find out in ways that go beyond guessing.

HOW TO ACQUIRE THE
HARD-BOILED ATTITUDE

You have just read why the mail-order man's experience evokes this hard-boiled attitude—and how he puts it to work. How can the general copywriter acquire it? And by "general" I mean the copywriter who does not have the benefit of knowing the number of sales his copy is producing; who, lacking such figures for each advertisement, rests his case upon his sincere conviction that he has done a conscientious and persuasive copy job and thus has a justifiable faith in its selling effectiveness.

Now, as Mizner said, "I respect faith, but doubt is what gets you an education." And doubt is one of the traits inherent in the hard-boiled attitude. Another (and one which stems from it) is the birth, care, and feeding of "the inquiring mind."

"Modest doubt is called the beacon of the wise." So says Shakespeare. Doubt is a good beacon for copy men too because it can stimulate and bring about the writing of advertisements of greater resultfulness. For when doubt enters the copywriter's mind, complacency must necessarily fly out. And complacency is an enemy of good copywriting.

One of the salutary services which doubt renders to the copy-writer is to pull him up short and make him wonder whether he can't make the copy in his advertisements work even harder. For it is daily apparent to any copywriter who is on the ball that advertisements could do more work than many advertisers ever make them do, or even try to make them do. As to the tremendous potential power of copy, such advertisers are "men of little faith." And to expect too little of copy is really to belittle it!

Doubt Makes Demands

Doubt thus impels the copy man to take the first giant step toward better copy—by making him more demanding about his own work. It brings him to a fuller realization that the more completely his advertisement—*on its own*—sells the reader, the nearer and quicker it will get that reader to the sales counter. And this realization can lead to the kind of critical analysis that is typical of a more hard-boiled attitude toward advertising. Here, for example, are just a few of the challenges presented by such analysis:

> *Brand Switching*—Is my ad convincing enough to make people insist, "I want that product and no other"?
>
> *Poor Dealer-Distribution*—Is my advertising persuasive enough to create the insistent consumer demand that would automatically increase distribution?
>
> *Weak Dealer-Co-operation*—How can a retailer be anything but lukewarm about the product if this copy of mine does not produce an active demand at his own counter?
>
> *Incapable Salesmanship at the Counter*—Can I shift more of the selling burden to the shoulders of my copy, a factor which *I* control?
>
> *Unfavorable Price Comparison*—If so, then the advertising I write must contain more "reason why" to help offset this competitive disadvantage.

A Hair Shirt Worth Wearing

Therefore, as you can see, the habit of doubt is a symptom of the acquisition of the hard-boiled attitude. It is one of the hair shirts that can make a copywriter scratch harder in his efforts to construct a more resultful advertisement. And from the habit of doubt stems the development of one of the other attributes of the hard-boiled attitude: the inquiring mind.

I must, however, admit that this quality, if carried to the gadfly extreme of a Socrates, is not always popular in one's own business circle. The light it can throw upon certain accepted procedures is sometimes inclined to be too glaringly revealing, too upsetting, too evidential of past error. But I am not suggesting that you contentiously don the iconoclastic mantle of a Socrates, Darwin, Vesalius, Galileo, or Copernicus. I am merely advocating the purposeful development of the inquiring mind—in order to do a relatively simple advertising job, one not earth-shaking in its impact or import. And that job is simply to try to cut down the margin between pure guesswork and copy that stands a better chance of proving that it can sell more goods or services, and doing so at less cost.

Not What They Think, but What They Do

Now, to summarize, how will these two traits, the habit of doubt and the inquiring mind, help you to achieve this purpose *for application in your own daily work?* First, and speaking generally, it will help you to avoid placing undue credence, or unsupported dependence, upon what Dr. H. C. Link called "the old psychology of advertising." Here is how he defines it:

> The old psychology was a study of *how* the mind *thinks;* the new psychology is a study of how the mind *acts.* The old psychology of advertising, for example, concerned itself with discovering what people thought about certain advertisements—which had the strongest appeal, the most effective copy, the greatest interest value, the best attention value, etc.

The new psychology is concerned with discovering what advertisements are most effective in getting people to buy. Not what people think, or *think* they think, but what they actually *do* about certain advertisements is the important question.

Second, the habit of doubt will impel you to become more searching and analytical in reaching a frank and realistic estimate of the hard-core selling ability of your own copy. That is a primary step toward achieving the improvement at which all the many suggestions given in this book are aimed.

Third, and speaking more specifically, the inquiring mind will provide you with the food of fact necessary to build up the selling stature of your copy. The kind of facts first to obtain—and then *to use*—are, however, not by any means confined to those mentioned in Chapters 3, 6 and various others in this book. They can come out of your own past and present experience—*if* your inquiring mind is constantly alert in seeking, seizing, and buttressing your copy with them.

Fourth, even though your work may not encompass the guidance supplied by such factors as records of mail-order results or department store and retail shelf-count sales figures, you can acquire—through the application of the two personal qualities described in this chapter—the advantages of the hard-boiled attitude. And this kind of approach to any advertising problem, regardless of its nature, will add to the extent and value of your accomplishment on every advertising job you are ever called upon to do.

QUIZ ON CHAPTER 13

1. What is meant by the "hard-boiled attitude"?

2. What is the acid test of a good ad?

3. What is the value of "negative knowledge"?

4. Which two traits in a copywriter can result in more effective work?

5. How can any copywriter acquire this hard-boiled attitude?

CHAPTER 14

RANDOM OBSERVATIONS

Several score of personal reflections based upon notes jotted down over the years . . . about copywriting, advertising, research, competition, and related subjects. Whether there may be any pearls for you in these little oysters of observation their author cannot say; he can only hope they at least contain some measure of mental nourishment.

"Only a mediocre writer is always at his best," Somerset Maugham tells us. As the saying goes, even "Homer nodded" and Shakespeare's genius sometimes sleeps soundly in his pages. But most of the fine writers in every field, including copywriting, have one thing in common: they worked hard and wrote much. Their tireless industry produced a quantity of acceptably good work. And out of this practice and experience came flashes of *exceptional* work, shot through with insight and effectiveness. Out of quantity came quality. "Inspiration," said Tennyson, "comes after effort."

★ ★ ★ ★

Herodotus, the Greek historian, writes that "Whatever a man has been thinking of during the day is wont to hover around him in the visions of his dreams at night." If he had been a copywriter he would have used the "fireless cooker" of his subconscious to solve some of his copy problems. Many a tough job of copywriting can be solved by the practice of utilizing the subconscious: by reviewing the difficulties before retiring at night. Very often, one awakes with the perfect copy approach, the long-sought headline. Sir Walter Scott, Alexander Graham Bell, Maeterlinck, Berlioz, and many other innovators thus intentionally put the subconscious to work. Worry over copy problems, by depending upon the conscious mind alone, can stop you from solving the very problems you are worrying about.

★ ★ ★ ★

The committee, or group, method of operation, with frequent and interminable meetings, reminds me of the remark by Napoleon: "How can any one make war through a council of war? If at two in the morning a good idea enters my mind, in a quarter of an hour I have issued my orders, and half an hour later my outposts are executing it." While ten minds can be discussing (and befogging) an advertising copy problem, one clear one can often not only solve it but be composing an advertisement putting it successfully into practice. "A dozen frowning faces around the conference table," says Ivan Veit of the *New York Times,* "are no substitute for one lonely guy struggling at his typewriter or layout pad."

★ ★ ★ ★

Bob Updegraff, in his classic of business, *Obvious Adams,* tells the story of one copywriter and idea man whose tremendous success was built upon what ex-Secretary of the Treasury George M. Humphrey called "an ability to see the obvious and do it." Adams never discarded an idea because it was "too obvious" *unless* there was some other good reason for tossing it aside. His thinking was never circuitous or indirect. His mind pierced through the miasma of irrelevancies and minor sales angles—and focused upon what would later prove to be the most motivational selling idea. "It was so darned obvious!" his clients probably thought to themselves. "Why didn't *I* ever think of it?" Why? Because, as Macauley said, "The more obvious things seem to wear transparent cloaks. We lose sight of them, simply because we know them so well."

★ ★ ★ ★

"Nothing in this world," says Victor Hugo, "is so powerful as an idea whose time has come." How often we find this true in copywriting! Brilliant copy can be written about a product—and nothing whatever happens after the copy runs. Yet mediocre, or even poor, copy can be written about another product, one with built-in desirability—and it starts a torrent of sales. To quote Rosser Reeves: "A gifted product is mightier than a gifted pen."

★ ★ ★ ★

In the writing of copy the appeal of "fear of loss" can often far outweigh the appeal of "the desire for gain." I have known men who refused to risk any amount of money in gambling—simply because the only amount of money that would give them any considerable kick in winning would have had to be sizeable enough to distress them greatly if they were to lose it. That is why good copy often utilizes both arguments: what you may lose, risk, or waste if you do not buy the product; and what you may gain or save if you do buy it.

★ ★ ★ ★

What is the best way for a copywriter to get going in the morning? It depends entirely upon the individual. I know of one unusual writer who keeps a list of the jobs he plans to do; then he tackles each one in rotation, not starting another until he has finished the preceding one. Another writer always, when possible, leaves part of a job undone until the next morning. Then he does not find it so hard to continue on a job he has already started. Still another says, "I have a formula for getting an ad written. The fact is, I don't like to write but I do like to edit. Therefore, I write swiftly and get my thoughts on paper somehow. After that the job is merely editing."

★ ★ ★ ★

A copywriter who grossly exaggerates the merits of a product should realize that the reaction of the purchaser can be so strong as to make him refuse ever to buy any product put out by that manufacturer. This resentment can reach a point which reminds me of one of the most powerful passages I have ever read. Achilles is talking, in the *Iliad* of Homer, to Odysseus about Agamemnon: "He cheated me and he did me hurt. Let him not beguile me with words again. This is enough for him. Let him of his own will be damned, since Zeus has taken his wits away from him. I hate his gifts. I hold him light as the strip of a splinter."

★ ★ ★ ★

To try to bludgeon your reader into a purchase reminds me of the story of the father of Frederick the Great. He noticed that his subjects were dodging him in the streets. So he struck one of them with his whip and cried, "Damn it, I want you to love me!" But I *have* heard of successful copy appeals based upon sheer effrontery. A certain much-used form letter, for example, from an insurance company assumes and expects action so positively that it simply asks for one's name, address, and age so that it may send information about a policy. That is all there is to the letter; but it is so positive, so expectant, and even so peremptory that it evidently gets the action it demands. And there was once much talk about an ad which had a headline, "Last Chance to Send $1." It is said that this drew many dollar bills—until the Post Office Department stepped in. The copy gave no reason for sending the dollar; nor did it promise to deliver anything for it. It simply traded upon brash effrontery and, to say the least, a positive approach.

★ ★ ★ ★

Copywriters constantly harassed by an advertiser's advice on how to write the copy about his product will enjoy the story of Lincoln after he had just received a long letter from General McClellan, advising him on how to carry on the nation's affairs.

"What did you reply?" someone asked Lincoln.

"Nothing," he said. "But it made me think of the Irishman whose horse kicked up and caught his hoof in the stirrup. 'Arrah!' said he. 'If *you* are going to get on, *I* will get off!' " Many a copywriter has often wished he could make that reply to an advertiser.

★ ★ ★ ★

I once knew an advertiser who had built up such a business and who had been operating for so many years that he was able to get out a booklet containing a list of customers in practically every county in the nation. It was particularly effective because it had the virtue of localization, that proof that the product had been purchased by neighbors of the prospect. In the use of testimonials, it is wise, whenever possible, to localize them. What happens to your neighbors ranks next in interest to the affairs of yourself and your family.

★ ★ ★ ★

The direct response to a mail-order advertisement very seldom runs higher than one half of one per cent of the total circulation of the publication—that is, up to five responses for every one thousand of the circulation. So, although yours may not be a mail-order ad, do not feel that after you have run it a few times you should retire it forever. If it has proven effective, keep running it; then, as with a race horse, breed it to other sales ideas to see if you can find new advertisements which will break the sales record of the first one. Blend in the appeals that you *know* are winners with new appeals which your experience indicates *may* be winners. That is the way to breed a new champion. Then keep running *that* one as long as your figures indicate it is doing a good sales job. Remember: neither you nor the advertiser should get bored with seeing and running any ad *unless* you have proof that the public is too!

★ ★ ★ ★

Some advertisers are so obsessed by what they think their competitors may be planning or doing that their every move is hamstrung or diluted by this fixation. It reminds me of two quotations about Napoleon. "He always gives his horse rein, and never troubles about what may be happening in his rear." And, concerning worries about a competitor's resources, "My calculations are based on more exact data, upon mathematical inferences. In the last resort, no one has more than he CAN have."

When somebody asked Willie Hoppe's manager how it was that Willie always won his billiard matches, the answer was: "Willie is always playing billiards; his competitors are always playing Willie."

★ ★ ★ ★

Some degree of success in writing for a high-school or college publication has often led a young person to believe he could achieve a great career in copywriting. Why this has sometimes proven to be a tragic error of judgment is explained in this quotation from Somerset Maugham's *The Summing Up:*

Youth is the inspiration. One of the tragedies of the arts is the spectacle of the vast number of persons who have been misled by this passing fertility to devote their lives to the effort of creation. Their invention deserts them as they grow older, and they are faced with the long years before them in which, unfitted by now for a more humdrum calling, they harass their wearied brain to beat out material it is incapable of giving them.

There seems to be a tendency among advertising people to read into readership ratings a lot more than they can tell. These ratings can provide a good gauge of how well an ad was read. Rating figures are indicators of readership and *as such* are significant and useful.

But high readership ratings are *not* proof of the *selling* ability of the advertisements so rated—unless substantiated by sales figures.

To make a comparison: One salesman can make twice as many calls as another—and still get fewer orders. Similarly, advertising campaigns have been run on the same product in which one series of advertisements with a relatively high readership rating showed a modest increase in sales; whereas another series with a much lower rating showed a much higher sales increase.

One series had greater readership, but the other had stronger salesmanship. One had more readers, yet got less sales action from this greater total than the other got from its smaller total.

So that the word "readership" doesn't become "reader(wor)ship" in your mind, the question you, as an advertising writer, want the answer to is—What did people *do* about it . . . *besides read?*

★ ★ ★ ★

As you leaf through page after page of advertisements in a magazine they seem to have a tendency to neutralize the effectiveness of each other. Why? If you were asked to give your answer in a few words you would probably conclude that almost every one looked too much like an ad—a carefully calculated, professional job of copywriting and layout-making.

Then suddenly you sometimes come upon an advertisement which doesn't seem to have that word stamped all over it. It has a non-professional appearance of spontaneity. It reads as though the advertiser has a genuinely helpful message for you; that, knowing better than anyone else the merits of his product, he might have sat down and written it himself.

The next time you see an advertisement which does not look so much like a professionally built, technically contrived effort to sell, clip it out for your scrapbook. It's worth some study.

★ ★ ★ ★

"Take Me Out to the Ball Game!" Good copywriters make it a habit to watch the reactions of people in the mass—and then to tie their observations up with the job of trying to write more effective advertising. Here are some "baseball tie-ups" that one might observe:

1. If a fan's favorite team wins a game he wants to read long accounts about it, but if it loses he is inclined to read only the head-line and perhaps a sentence or two. (If your copy keeps making the product win advantages and consumer benefits for people, won't they read it more thoroughly?)

2. Fans like to read all about the very game they have just seen— because it is then within their own personal experience ("Belief is a fabric of personal experiences." So when trying to prove claims, among your facts introduce some which will make the reader say, "Yes, I *know* that's a fact!")

3. The crowd doesn't care what *form* the pitcher displays. What *results* is he going to get with it? (Avoid the common error of relying on form instead of on substance.)

4. During the War Bond Drives at the ball games many people were amazed at the big pledges yelled out by individuals from the general grandstands, and even from the bleachers. (In *any* medium of mass circulation there are many people able to buy anything your copy makes them want badly enough.)

★ ★ ★ ★

Here are some chapter titles from two well-known books: *How to Win Friends and Influence People* and *Strategy in Handling People:*

> Six Ways to Make People Like You
> Do This and You'll Be Welcome Anywhere
> Right and Wrong Methods of Praising People
> An Easy Way to Become a Good Conversationalist
> The Knack of Getting Co-operation
> Three Successful Salesman and Their One Secret
> Things to Look For in Judging People

★ ★ ★ ★

They'd make irresistible ad headlines, wouldn't they? Note how specific each one is, the reward for reading which each one promises. There is surely a lesson here for copywriters!

What's wrong with this advertising headline and subhead about a certain book by an authority, telling women how to make hats?

New Easy Way to Make,
Trim, and Remake Your Own Hats
How any woman can now
have $7.50 hats for only
$1.50—$5.00 hats for
less than $1.00

★ ★ ★ ★

It seems to me that its basic fault is this: It puts the *reader* to work right away—instead of putting the product to work for the reader in accomplishing the END RESULT she wants. The main headline doesn't paint any picture of what she can get; it first tells her what she has to do to get it.

And *that* can really come later; it is part of the product story. After you have created a strong desire on her part to gain the result which the product offers, you can then tell her how that result can be accomplished.

Now how can we recast the headline and subhead to make the whole idea more attractive to the reader? What does she want most, as far as hats are concerned? What's the strongest appeal to her? Suppose we revise the headline and subhead to something like this:

Now You Can Have
Twice as Many New Hats!
—for such perfectly ridiculous amounts as only 50 cents, 75 cents, $1.25 each. And they'll be smart, expensive-looking hats, too— "Dream Hats"—the envy of every woman you know!

★ ★ ★ ★

And then suppose, in the first paragraphs of our body matter, we don't begin to talk right away about what our reader has to *do* in order to sit down to this hat feast. Instead, let us etch a little deeper the picture portrayed in the new headline and subhead. The first two paragraphs might be somewhat as follows:

Now you may have more new hats than you ever dreamed possible —and on your present hat budget. Smart-looking, becoming, attractive hats, for every hair-do and for every occasion. For morning, afternoon, and evening; for parties, formal or informal; for shopping, bridge, cocktails, tea, or church.

And not the sort of hats that you would "meet yourself coming down the street in." But hats with "flair" and inspiration that will bring out your best points as a woman of individuality and charm.

★ ★ ★ ★

Certain passages in this book refer to the fact that good copy based upon a strong appeal can successfully hurdle dealer obstacles and turn in a noteworthy job in spite of them. I want to cite an example of this, one with which I was personally familiar.

A new product was being promoted in a fiercely competitive field. The advertiser's test campaign in various areas (the only ones in which he already had distributors) produced truly sensational results. In fact, they were so excellent that he decided to make a daring experiment.

This advertiser's normal procedure would naturally have been to first contact selected dealers in certain new areas and line them up as distributors—*before* releasing the local advertising campaign. Instead, he deliberately shipped them an introductory supply of the product entirely on consignment—but timing the operation carefully so that the advertising ran the same day they received their shipments.

It worked. The advertising (as had happened in the previous test areas) at once began producing calls in volume at the dealers' counters. So, in order not to lose these sales, they opened their shipments and started selling the product. This plan of making the already-proven strength of the advertising achieve "automatic" distribution as well as sales was later used throughout the country.

I wouldn't say that this rather highhanded procedure did not arouse some resentment. But that was drowned out by the pain-relieving clamor of the dealers' cash registers.

★ ★ ★ ★

Sometimes it is difficult to decide which is the major selling appeal of a product—which one, or ones, to feature.

When you face such a problem (and have no guidance from previous experience) it is often wise to "merchandise" the product from many angles, stressing as many different advantages as you can think of, "letting the chips fall where they may." By doing so, you'll let the reader determine for himself which advantages have the most appeal in relation to his individual circumstances and requirements. And you don't go out on a limb by basing your entire advertisement on one or two selling appeals which may actually be weak in attractiveness. This strategy puts into use a principle Harry Overstreet mentions: "This secret of all true persuasion is to induce the person to persuade himself."

★ ★ ★ ★

"Our creators of advertising today," said Jim Young, "either never had, or have largely lost, the art of making small space pay." The writing of small space ads is sometimes looked upon by big-time copywriters as more of an insult than a challenge. For it is a challenge—and one that has cheerfully been accepted by the many copywriters in the past who have used small space to build big businesses.

But, as James D. Woolf wrote, "Nobody in 'big time' pays much attention to these small advertisers. They are seldom awarded 'Oscars' at advertising shows. Few textbooks on advertising devote much scholarly consideration to them. Quietly and unobstrusively, asking for no applause, the small advertiser tends to his own knitting, wastes no time making speeches at ad conventions."

Also, it is a good idea, when you have a large advertisement to write, to write it first as a small one. This will get you right down to the strongest basic appeals. Since you are confining your sales talk to small space you will have to give each copy point the acid test. And you will find that when you get to building the smaller ad into larger space it will become a more powerful selling job than if you had rattled around in large space as a starter.

Over the years many advertisers have developed a whole stable of small ads of proven effectiveness. They run them time after time and all over the place. No destruction of merchandise or premises due to fire, flood, or earthquake can put such advertisers out of business. They can always trot these front-runner ponies out of the stable and start all over again.

The march of the body copy in an advertisement can often be bogged down by solid paragraphs describing the physical specifications of the product. This interferes with the sequential flow of the copy, causing the reader to lose interest.

A good way to present such material (which your more interested prospects *do* want to know) is to relegate it to a panel in the advertisement. Then it is there for those who wish this information; but it does not slow up your presentation of the more motivating and dynamic body copy telling about the end-result advantages of purchasing the product.

★ ★ ★ ★

Direct Mail Advice for the Advertiser: Unless you can talk personally with all the people on your prospect list, direct mail is the least expensive, most effective, and most direct way to tell your story to them individually. But there are three essentials to greatest possible success. If you don't observe these three rules direct mail can be a disastrous failure. Here they are:

1. *Careful and Continuous Assembling of Your Prospect List.* Don't put "any old name" on your prospect list in the mistaken belief that "the more names you use the better net result you will get." Build your list carefully and continuously. Do not spend mailing money on prospects living in neighborhoods or circumstances which make their favorable response to your proposition extremely unlikely. On the contrary, add to your list the names of people in neighborhoods of the kind from which you *now* get your most profitable business.

Follow up old customers with offerings they have not taken advantage of before. And, after you have made a satisfied customer, use this contact as a means of mailing to other good names your customer suggests or recommends.

2. *Use Good Material for Your Circularizing Work.* Don't send out literature which does not do full justice to your proposition and to the quality of the service you render.

3. *Make a Consistent Planned Program of Your Direct Mail Work.* One of the greatest pitfalls in direct mail is the habit of doing it in a hit-or-miss fashion, "shooting out a mailing when you get time." Direct mail can be a major source of profit for you—but not

unless you plan it carefully and carry out your plan on a predetermined systematic basis. Plan your program ahead for a full year—bearing in mind the seasonal variations which affect your business, and scheduling your mailings so that you can cash in most profitably during the periods when there is the greatest natural activity in relation to the offering you are making.

Don't treat direct mail as a stepchild. Chart it carefully in advance—designating how many prospects (or old customers) you are going to mail to, what pieces you are going to send, and to whom you are going to send them.

These are three of the primary requirements for successful direct-mail operation. Much time, work, and money can be lost by haphazard, casual, sporadic attention to this selling method. Large profits can be gained by adopting, and staying with, an intelligent program—using good lists, adding to them carefully and constantly; mailing effective sales literature which has been successfully tested; and getting your mailings out systematically, even if you have to work many hours overtime in order to meet the due date you have scheduled on your direct-mail chart.

★ ★ ★ ★

You have doubtless many times thrown away a piece of direct-mail literature—and wondered how such advertising could possibly pay. Yet the successful mailer knows that a large percentage of those who receive it will do just as you have done. But, if it is properly prepared and tested, it will get action from a sufficiently profitable percentage of those who receive it.

And that is all you can work toward in your space advertising. If you can get only a relatively small percentage of the total circulation of your medium to act upon your message your copy can be enormously successful. As Walter Weir says,

> It is always better to have a few people read your advertisement and buy your product then to have a lot of them read it and do nothing about it. I am frequently amazed that an advertiser who will not tolerate waste circulation in a newspaper or a magazine schedule will not always apply the same criterion to his advertising message. He wants a lot of people to read it, regardless of whether they are

actually prospects for his product. It's one of the many mysteries of this business.

★ ★ ★ ★

And so it comes down to the question of whether you want readership by the many more than you want "actionship" from a much smaller number. "Might we perhaps," queries John De Wolf, of the G. M. Basford Company, "induce more action by forgetting 99% of the readers and really working on the 1% whose attention we can catch with mail-order headlines and very long copy? Why shouldn't such techniques work when our objective is to get relatively few readers to do something specific?"

Of course, as mentioned elsewhere in this book, this philosophy is not applicable to the sale of every article; such, for example, as those involving no serious decision or sizable expenditure. But it does apply in numberless other instances where the advertiser, instead of merely hoping for widespread readership, could improve his copy to such an extent that it would not only be interesting enough to be read by many but persuasive enough to be acted upon by some.

★ ★ ★ ★

The above considerations lead to one answer as to why mail-order advertisements with a proven record of effectiveness so often receive a very poor readership rating. It is probably because most *non*mail-order advertisements usually try to gain as thorough reading as possible from as many readers as possible. On the contrary, mail-order advertisements are usually more selective in their appeal (thus sacrificing quantity readership) and are designed to produce immediate action from this more limited readership. In other words, the mail-order ad does not seek quantity of readership *per se*. It will gladly sacrifice that in order to gain a reading so thorough as to induce as many readers as possible to take action.

★ ★ ★ ★

"Man's inhumanity to man." I have often been distressed at how little regard even creative men have for the work of other creative men. In the field of copywriting, they themselves know through their own arduous experience how much hour-after-hour toil can be put into a copy job. Yet they will sometimes wade into a subordinate's copy mercilessly, not constructively or helpfully but seemingly for the sadistic satisfaction of tearing it apart. They may glance over it casually and toss it aside, without any attempt to understand the reasoning behind it. Or, without any valid reason, they may joyfully start slashing it up immediately, apparently because their own sweat did not go into its conception.

I know that psychologists have a good explanation for the reasons behind this "slaughter of the innocents," and I can well understand why noncreative advertising "experts" enjoy the compensating consolation of this method of self-assertion. But that cannot make it any the less disheartening.

In extenuation, one may say that this blue-pencil mania is not always intentionally homicidal. It is sometimes simply due to a congenital fear or antipathy for a copy approach considered too off-beat or unusual, even though the directive on the job may really have been to "do something entirely new and different." Or it may merely be the manifestation of an ingrained habit of negation; an instinctive no response that, in all fairness, may be neither capricious nor deliberately vindictive but which actually, in many cases, stems from the basic human frailty described by the poet Stephen Vincent Benét:

> The fault is no decisive, villainous knife
> But the dull saw that is the routine mind.

★ ★ ★ ★

The Age of Inquiry in Advertising. Even though the accuracy of certain research procedures may later be disproved they serve a worth-while purpose if they stimulate the development of further, and more scientific, research. Certainties as to advertising response may never be uncovered; but sounder and more dependable procedures of inquiry and research will surely be ultimately developed. If conducted with integrity and impartiality, who can quibble too much about the procedures of the researchers as being too broad, too narrow, too theoretical? Other fields of inquiry, into subjects once considered too irrational and nonabsolute for true scientific analysis, have finally yielded a rich and dependable harvest of practical guidance.

Considering the billions that are spent each year upon advertising, we can well go along with any intelligent methods of research which, in the long run or short, promise to cut down some of the waste. John Wanamaker said he knew that half of the money he spent for advertising was being wasted—but that he didn't know which half. Perhaps researchers will someday be able to provide an answer.

★ ★ ★ ★

Some years ago, in the Creative Man's Corner of *Advertising Age,* I read this remark: "When an advertiser has a product he knows is going to appeal to only a limited audience, he seems to employ much sounder thinking than when he pushes a product that can be bought by all and sundry."

As a shining example of a bull's-eye approach read this 28-line want ad:

WANTED—A pleasant woman, middle-aged, and free of domestic responsibilities to apply her knowledge and help to the task of operating our home in the comfortable manner to which we are accustomed. We are not expecting to hire a mule, so that my wife can sit in an easy chair and watch her work. The lady of our house is quite capable and humble enough to do her share, but she does need help. We have two children who are no better or no worse than the average, and I can personally guarantee their good behavior, with word or rod. For the woman who answers these qualifications we can provide her with money, a private room and bath, and all the respect, comfort and security of a member of our family, thru health and illness, not only for life but forever!

★ ★ ★ ★

How pallid is most advertising copy—compared with this! From a copy standpoint, remember constantly that even though a publication may have a multimillion circulation your advertisement is talking to only one person at a time.

★ ★ ★ ★

Don't sell punctuation short! It is really a highly important (though commonly underestimated) factor in the writing of good advertising copy. When you realize the cost of advertising space, a piece of copy can represent a great deal of money *per word.* Yet these words and sentences and paragraphs cannot get as careful and thorough a reading, and cannot be plainly understood, if punctuation is careless, incorrect, or missing entirely when it is needed for clarity.

Large sums are actually wasted because many advertising writers do not fully realize the extent to which punctuation—and punctuation alone—can make or break the readership of an advertisement. It's no small expense to an advertiser when his copy is so casully or improperly punctuated that it loses the interest and results in the confusion of a large percentage of the readers he has paid so much to reach.

Another thing: Punctuation can be an active and not merely a passive factor in writing. For example, among the jobs of a copy chief whom I know is the editing of copy in which the writer briefly outlines the plots of mystery novels so that people will want to buy them. He is often amazed at how the simple repunctuation of these pieces of copy can improve them. The more judicious use of exclamation points, dashes, semicolons, colons, a series of three or four periods in a row—coupled with simpler and shorter sentence structure and the elimination of dangling clauses—can retain and heighten interest, increase suspense, build up dramatic climaxes . . . and sell more books.

Properly handled, your punctuation can do a bigger job for you than you may imagine. It is obvious that you need it for clarity; but, beyond that, it can help you immeasurably in holding the interest you have captured, in putting more impact and punch into your writing, and in conveying people more smoothly and tractably along the road your copy is traveling toward winning a favorable opinion of what you are and a yes response to what you want them to do.

There are many good stories illustrating how faulty punctuation (or the lack of any) can result in confusion, indefiniteness, or misunderstanding. This one points up its potentialities for ambiguity. While the playwright Richard Brinsley Sheridan was a member of the British Parliament, he was once called upon to apologize to a fellow member. He rose and said: "Mr. Speaker I said the honorable member was a liar it is true and I am sorry for it," adding that the honorable member could place the punctuation marks where he pleased.

Every copy man should sometime write a want ad. When you do one for yourself—and want to make sure your money is well spent—you will really concentrate upon every word you put into it. You'll pack it with persuasive facts. And, if you are wise, you will make it long enough to bring you the result you are paying by the word to get.

Stuart D. Cowan, Jr., tells of a copywriter friend who wrote a want ad which pulled so many good responses that his reaction was this:

I think every young copy writer should write at least one classified ad and stick it in a magazine or newspaper—even if he's selling an old lamp or a stamp album. The ring of the telephone, or letters from the postman, will sell him on advertising like nothing else on earth.

Now I sit down at my desk at the office each morning with a burning desire to write good copy. I get out and talk to the people who read my stuff—jobbers, dealers, consumers. I want to see letters, coupons, sales figures—results! I want my copy to sell!

Think of some of the gorgeous full-color travel ads you have seen. Then read this little want ad that cost only a few dollars:

Mexico $80 a Month
per person. Includes food, liquor, cigarettes, your own three bedroom furnished house and patio, cook, maid, and 17 ft. sloop on magnificent Lake Chapala. English American artist colony in fishing village. Winter temp. 75, summer 85. Write ———.

★ ★ ★ ★

"Just knock the copy out; it shouldn't be too big a job." It always gives a copywriter an acute pain when someone (perhaps someone who can't construct a good clear sentence) asks him to dash off a piece of copy. It makes it all sound so simple. A good basic idea for the ad can be pulled right out of the air; they're a dime a dozen. Just the right headline pops out of the typewriter. The body matter pours out automatically, line after line. It's just a pushover—for the other fellow. It could be amusing, but it never is.

"A single word has sometimes lost or won an empire. . . . " This well-known quotation brings to mind a scene all too common when a copywriter waits while an advertiser goes over a piece of copy. Suddenly the advertiser fixes upon one single word, often in the headline. He does not like that one word, but definitely. His violent disapproval of it subconsciously starts a whole sequence of nega-tion. His chain reaction is to find other complaints concerning the copy. The finale: N.G., down the drain.

And that's not an exaggeration. For I have seen many a good piece of copy rejected because of a single word or phrase. The unhappy copywriter, try as he may, cannot seem to get around this 8-ball. It does no good to suggest synonyms. It's too late; the advertiser has already taken an inflexible no position on the whole job.

This is just one of the experiences that can knock the sensitive mental and emotional apparatus of a good copywriter out of kilter. "Because he is sensitive," writes Walter Weir, "he magnifies things. (Or perhaps because he magnifies things, he is sensitive. It doesn't matter.) He has a more lively imagination than the average person and occasionally sees things that less imaginative persons do not see. . . . The little emotional wheels and cogs by which he works are worth some attention—and occasionally some oil. Suppose he *is* a sensitive soul? He's got to be if he's good."

★ ★ ★ ★

"Use words to paint a picture," the copywriter is always ad-monished. And rightly so. Here is a short but instructive example of what a difference just a few words can make when conveying the same idea.

As a parent, how wonderful it will be if, when the time comes, *your* boy or girl is accepted by the college of your choice—no matter how many other students apply for admission!

Now, with a change of four or five words, we have this:

As a parent, how wonderful it will be if, when the time comes, the college of your choice opens wide its doors to *your* boy or girl—no matter how many other students are clamoring for admission!

One salesman may call on a prospect five times before closing the sale. Another salesman, with a different presentation, may call once—and get the order. Similarly, one advertising appeal may appear five times and yet produce no more business than a different copy appeal produces from one insertion.

How can an advertiser find the appeal that will make his appropriation do a bigger job in a shorter time? Actually, no one can tell you with any certainty in the *beginning* except those who always determine in the *end*—the readers who pass judgment by either buying or not buying.

★ ★ ★ ★

Some years ago the magazines were filled with what were called "narrative" ads. These were delightful little tales about the experiences of imaginary people. Some of these ads were highly successful, even though the incidents portrayed were totally incredible. For example, how Joe Doaks (in practically no time) developed such a phenomenal memory that he quickly took over his boss's job—with his former boss pleading with him to re-employ him in *any* job, regardless of how menial. Or how Plain Jane Brown acquired (with almost no effort) such a gorgeous complexion that all the men who had previously shunned her were soon groveling at her feet. Etc., etc., *ad infinitum.*

I know of an advertiser who resurrected one such narrative ad. It had been so successful that it had been run profitably in a quarter of a million dollars worth of space. It had been *the* ad, the proven best among a whole stable of ads which had worked out well. Years later, this advertiser tested the same advertisement in a number of publications. Wherever it ran it was now a total flop! The desires of people had not changed, because other types of advertisement offering the same product worked satisfactorily. But people's reservoir of credibility had gone down over the years; their faculty of belief could no longer swallow the narrative portrayed.

★ ★ ★ ★

Bearing in mind the five fundamentals described in this book, let us make an interesting analysis. Before us is a full-page newspaper advertisement. It is a good job—except in one vital respect. In fact, all of the ads in the campaign do a fine copy job but for this single element.

The ad captures the attention of those it is trying to reach. It contains somewhere between 500 and 750 words of exceptionally good copy. This copy presents persuasively the many advantages of buying the product. It offers convincing proof, in believable words and dramatic pictures. It handles excellently the first four of the five fundamentals discussed in this book. And then . . .

It ends up with merely the "go to your dealer" pull for action which is referred to as "The First Form" in Chapter 5. "What more could it do?" perhaps you say.

This advertiser has thousands of dealers. So I wonder why he couldn't have offered his readers some specific *extra* inducement to "go to your dealer" at once—so that the good intentions stimulated by the advertisement would not be so greatly dissipated by the attrition of procrastination and inertia. For example, he operates in a field where credit-card retail accounts are eagerly sought. Perhaps the advertisements might have concluded with a simple application form for one of these, to be presented at the dealer's for processing by the company. Useful and inexpensive little gimmicks are commonly distributed by companies in his field. So he might have made such an offer "if you go to one of our dealers promptly—while the supply lasts." He might have offered, obtainable at his dealers, a booklet filled with helpful information about saving time, money, or work in connection with the use of the product itself. Not merely more "sales talk" about the product (for his advertisement has already done a good job there) but desirable additional guidance that people would like to have.

Chapter 5 of this book gives other suggestions for "beefing up" the mere "go to your dealer" type of close. By giving the prospect a definite and attractive *reason* for taking the desired action you not only increase the ad's responsiveness but you can make it provide you with incontrovertible evidence as to how great that response has been.

Anyone who knows, respects, and applauds an otherwise fine piece of selling copy is bound to be disappointed if he finds that the last important factor is either not included at all or has been muffed—if the interest, conviction, and desire to purchase which have been so effectively stimulated are not cashed in on and motivated by the strongest possible bid for action.

★ ★ ★ ★

Steuart Henderson Britt, a psychologist and a director of research, has pointed out some principles of learning which are useful for a copywriter to know. Here are a few of them:

Points presented at the beginning and end of the message are remembered better than those in the middle.

Unpleasant things may sometimes be learned as readily as pleasant things, but the most ineffective stimuli are those which arouse little or no emotional response.

Things that are learned and understood tend to be better retained than things learned by rote.

It is easier to recognize something than it is to recall it.

Knowledge of results leads to increases in learning.

Learning is aided by active practice rather than passive reception.

A message is more easily learned and accepted if it does not interfere with earlier habits.

★ ★ ★ ★

Concerning the public utterances of President Martin Van Buren it was said that "he rowed to his object with muffled oars." We might liken this in some respects to one of two types of copywriter. The members of this school of writing are adept at a calm, reasoned approach. They undermine doubts and objections rather than attack them head-on. They bore under rather than blast through. Their approach is indirect but nevertheless they do arrive at their objective, achieving hard-sell impact by soft-sell techniques.

Their opposite numbers are the frontal-attack boys. They are as subtle as a bulldozer. They don't insinuate; they declare. They don't intimate; they assert. They do not try to excavate under doubt, so that it falls of its own weight; they smash into it with dynamic abandon.

The members of both schools can achieve good marks for resultful advertising. It depends upon the job to be done—and the skill of the doer.

●

What is so rare as a day—when an advertiser will stay with a copy angle which has demonstrated conclusively that it is doing a phenomenal sales job! The advertiser gets bored with it—long before the public shows any signs, saleswise, that it has done so. And so the word goes out to the advertising people: "Give us something brand new, completely different; totally unlike anything we have ever done before." Consequently, proven sales-makers are constantly being discarded.

When an experienced mail-order advertiser discovers something that works exceptionally well, he repeats it until the drop-off in result makes further repetition unprofitable. Then he takes the same basic idea and dishes it up in a different way. The core of the successful idea is retained; but it is changed unrecognizably through variations of headlines, copy treatment, layouts, and display elements. The cycle then starts all over again—until the fundamental appeal, no matter how presented, no longer seems to be worth further exploitation.

Sometimes the inherent strength of the appeal justifies an apparently endless series of permutations. Its universality endows it with perennial viability. So on and on it goes, in different forms, suggestive of Dora, the cow, which the novelist Thorne Smith wrote about: "If a cow drank milk it would be something like discovering perpetual motion."

★ ★ ★ ★

I have always been interested in the first reactions of copy men when the writing of an advertisement is assigned to them. The difference reminds me of the story of two shoe salesmen who had just arrived in Africa. One saw the shoeless natives of that particular part of Africa and he immediately wired his home office: NOBODY WEARS SHOES; AM RETURNING. The other salesman cabled: DOUBLE INITIAL ORDER; NOBODY HAS SHOES.

Likewise, one copywriter will at once think of the difficulties of the job at hand; the other will think of the opportunities. This does not mean that the first copywriter will not do a good job; sometimes it is quite the contrary. Its difficulties will often stimulate him to dig deeper and come up with an excellent piece of copy; whereas the other fellow, thinking it kind of a pushover, will give it the "once over lightly" treatment—and have to do it over again.

★ ★ ★ ★

"I don't know!" These three words are, it seems to me, too rarely used. The failure to use them courageously has often put advertising people out on such a shaky limb that they lost more face by later trying to scurry back than they would have if they had frankly admitted, "I don't know but I'll find out."

Faced with a direct query from an advertiser, such men will sometimes hazard a mere guess (as, for example, relative to probable cost or result). Later, the unforgetting advertiser may have a serious and entirely justifiable beef. The advertising business has become too complex for anyone to be expected to have all the answers at the tip of his tongue. In the long run, and even the short, sweet are the uses of . . . humility.

And, since we are on a moralizing binge, it can't do any harm also to point out that there are too many unknown and unprovable factors in advertising for its practitioners to ride roughshod over the viewpoints of others, even of those who might be called rank amateurs. Sometimes the instinctive selling sense of these nonprofessionals has confounded the experts—with a freshness and naïveté of approach that was handsomely rewarded by a buying public. Thomas Edison gave the answer to the professionally opinionated when he said, "The next time you are tempted to ignore the viewpoint of another person, remember, it is fairly unusual for anybody, or anything, to be 100% wrong. Even a stopped clock is right twice a day."

★ ★ ★ ★

As mentioned a few pages earlier, I am in favor of a never-ending Age of Inquiry in advertising. But that does not prevent me from pointing out that many sensationally resultful ads and campaigns were sparked long before the advertising world had any idea of the relationship to copywriting of such terms as "libido," "id," and "narcissism."

Some of these masterpieces of selling in print changed the buying habits of the nation. The master copywriters who created them had selling intuition that transcended the necessity for the guidance of psychological or psychiatric analysis. In fact, the work of these giants among copy men, regardless of when they were at the peak of their creativeness, can still be studied gainfully by the copy men of today —no matter how experienced or inexperienced he may be. (Who knows?—it might turn out as Coleridge said: "A dwarf sees farther than the giant when he has the giant's shoulder to mount on.")

At least some measure of this trait of intuition is present and active in all copywriters who are truly good craftsmen. Subconsciously it becomes part of the fabric of the ads they write. Often it can eliminate that testing of the obvious which is defined elsewhere in his book: "the superfluous confirmation of already-known and proved principles of why people react as they do, and just what stimuli make them do so."

I know of one interesting example of this. An advertiser had insisted upon a survey being made of the reaction of prospective customers to a certain sales talk. It was an expensive survey to make, involving calls at many homes. But before the survey was conducted, a group of copywriters of long and successful experience (who were also thoroughly familiar with the product and with this sales presentation) listed what they believed would be the response to each sales point—writing it in the words and expressions they thought the prospects would use during the interviews. Their papers were then put into the office safe; and they were not referred to again until the tabulated results of the survey were in.

What happened was not too remarkable—if you realize the acuteness of good copy men with an insight into the principles of human behavior and an instinct as to the probable reactions toward a product with which they are familiar. Their papers listed accurately the objections later raised by the prospective customers, interviewed. In almost the exact words used by the prospects, they reported in advance the remarks which these prospects actually made. Remarkable? No. For men with such a background, what was likely to happen was once foretold by Mark Twain: "It was wonderful to find America, but it would have been more wonderful to miss it."

In a way this whole subject reminds me of the story which Robert Keith Leavitt tells of how the mighty battleship *Missouri* ran aground when it was under the sole "Look, Ma, no hands" control of an elaborate complex of electronic sounding and ranging devices, robot course plotters, and digital computers. Yet one good, experienced sailor with a one-dollar chart in his hand could have kept her on course and out of trouble. In other words, in many fields of endeavor we pile Ossa upon Pelion. . . . We so often resort to complicated impedimenta and complex procedures to accomplish a simple purpose which one or two capable minds could readily achieve, without any fanfare or impressive stage properties.

★ ★ ★ ★

And now we come to the end of our book. Obviously, the study of the art of copywriting actually fans out into one justifying many volumes the size of ours. So, concerning the one you presently hold in your hand, I'll have to leave it up to you and Sam Weller's father: "Vether it's worth while goin' through so much to learn so little, as the charity-boy said ven he got to the end of the alphabet, is a matter o' taste." But I do hope you don't conclude, as Sam's father did, "*I* rayther think it isn't."

INDEX

ORIGINAL UNABRIDGED EDITION

THINK
AND
GROW
RICH

NAPOLEON HILL

FOREWORD BY
MELVIN POWERS

Original Unabridged Edition

THINK AND GROW RICH

by Napoleon Hill
Foreword by Melvin Powers

Millions of copies sold!

This book is one of the most prestigious and beloved in the field of motivational literature. It is a reprint of the original, unabridged, classic edition of *Think and Grow Rich* by Napoleon Hill, which has sold millions of copies in its various editions and has been translated into numerous languages. Everyone interested in the motivational field knows about this remarkable book that has helped shape the lives of millions of its readers.

In *Think and Grow Rich*, Napoleon Hill shares his brilliant philosophy and practical techniques for achieving your financial goals, reaching your highest potential, and ultimately creating a life that brings you great personal happiness. This book teaches you how to harness the awesome mental magic of your mind. You are given a blueprint for self-mastery. You learn there are no limitations to what you can accomplish; only those you impose on yourself.

Napoleon Hill said, "If you can conceive it, you can achieve it." This precept has proven true repeatedly throughout history. Did we not send a man to the moon and accomplish other seemingly miraculous feats in many fields of endeavor? Every one of these feats began as an idea that was then transformed into reality. *Think and Grow Rich* shows you how to transform your dreams into reality, too.

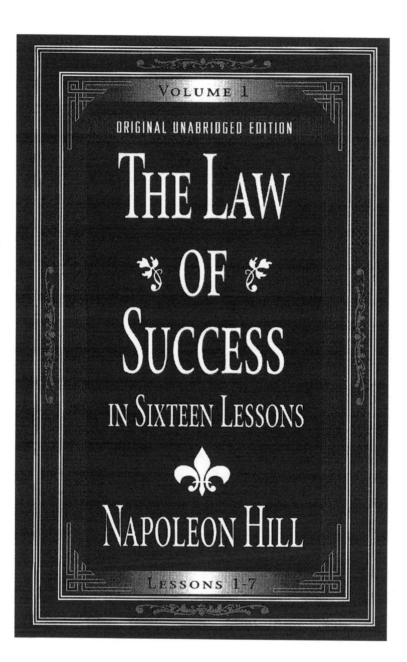

VOLUME 1

ORIGINAL UNABRIDGED EDITION

THE LAW OF SUCCESS

IN SIXTEEN LESSONS

NAPOLEON HILL

LESSONS 1-7

A personal word from the publisher, Melvin Powers

THE LAW OF SUCCESS IN SIXTEEN LESSONS

by Napoleon Hill

Over the years, Wilshire Book Company has sold more than seven million copies of *Think and Grow Rich* and has had thousands of requests from enthusiastic readers for Napoleon Hill's original eight-book series, *The Law of Success in Sixteen Lessons.*

After many years of intensive and extensive research, we found a set of the books in mint condition. We are excited to finally be republishing this original, unabridged, classic edition of the world famous series, reproduced just as it first appeared, and compiled into a convenient, beautiful two-volume set.

If your life has been enriched by Napoleon Hill's *Think and Grow Rich,* you'll love *The Law of Success in Sixteen Lessons.* It teaches the life-changing philosophy upon which *Think and Grow Rich* and most modern motivational books are based.

We have received accolades from all over the world for making Napoleon Hill's timeless words of wisdom available to enhance the lives of new generations. We know you'll be delighted with this two-volume treasure. It is a blueprint for success in any field of endeavor. You will learn how to think like a winner . . . be a winner . . . and reap the rewards of a winner. Now get ready for Napoleon Hill to help make your most cherished dreams come true.

Two-Volume Set

THREE MAGIC WORDS

by U.S. Andersen

Over 1,000,000 people have already learned an incredible, life-changing secret from this bestselling book.

Three Magic Words will bring you everything you ever wanted. Once you learn its message and understand the significance of it, your experience of living will be enriched every day.

This remarkable book unravels the mysteries of what we are, where we came from, why we are here, and where we are going. It shows how the universe works and how to harness its unlimited power—a force so strong that, once revealed to you, will grant you power over all things.

When you read *Three Magic Words* and do as it suggests, you cannot fail to accomplish what it promises.

I invite you to meet an extraordinary princess and accompany her on an enlightening journey. You will laugh with her and cry with her, learn with her and grow with her . . . and she will become a dear friend you will never forget.

Marcia Grad Powers

1 MILLION COPIES SOLD WORLDWIDE

The Princess Who Believed in Fairy Tales

"Here is a very special book that will guide you lovingly into a new way of thinking about yourself and your life so that the future will be filled with hope and love and song."

OG MANDINO
Author, *The Greatest Salesman in the World*

The Princess Who Believed in Fairy Tales by Marcia Grad is a personal growth book of the rarest kind. It's a delightful, humor-filled story you will experience so deeply that it can literally change your feelings about yourself, your relationships, and your life.

The princess's journey of self-discovery on the Path of Truth is an eye-opening, inspiring, empowering psychological and spiritual journey that symbolizes the one we all take through life as we separate illusion from reality, come to terms with our childhood dreams and pain, and discover who we really are and how life works.

If you have struggled with childhood pain, with feelings of not being good enough, with the loss of your dreams, or if you have been disappointed in your relationships, this book will prove to you that happy endings—and new beginnings—are always possible. Or, if you simply wish to get closer to your own truth, the princess will guide you.

The universal appeal of this book has resulted in its translation into numerous languages.

Excerpts from Readers' Heartfelt Letters

"*The Princess* is truly a gem! Though I've read a zillion self-help and spiritual books, I got more out of this one than from any other one I've ever read. It is just too illuminating and full of wisdom to ever be able to thank you enough. The friends and family I've given copies to have raved about it."

"*The Princess* is powerful, insightful, and beautifully written. I am seventy years old and have seldom encountered greater wisdom. I've been waiting to read this book my entire life. You are a psychologist, a guru, a saint, and an angel all wrapped up into one. I thank you with all my heart."

Available wherever books are sold or from **Wilshire Book Company**.
For our complete catalog or to order online, please visit **www.mpowers.com**

An Unforgettable Treasure of Laughter and Wisdom

THE KNIGHT IN RUSTY ARMOR

Over 4 million copies sold worldwide!

This story is guaranteed to captivate your imagination as it helps you discover the secret of what is most important in life. It's a delightful tale of a desperate knight in search of his true self.

Join him as he faces a life-changing dilemma upon discovering that he is trapped in his armor, just as we may be trapped in *our* armor—an invisible one we put on to protect ourselves from others and from various aspects of life.

As the knight searches for a way to free himself, he receives guidance from the wise sage Merlin the Magician, who encourages him to embark on the most difficult crusade of his life. The knight takes up the challenge and travels the Path of Truth, where he meets his real self for the first time and confronts the Universal Truths that govern his life—and ours.

The knight's journey reflects our own, filled with hope and despair, belief and disillusionment, laughter and tears. His insights become our insights as we follow along on his intriguing adventure of self-discovery. Anyone who has ever struggled with the meaning of life and love will discover profound wisdom and truth as this unique fantasy unfolds.

Robert Fisher's *The Knight in Rusty Armor* will expand your mind, touch your heart, and nourish your soul. It is one of Wilshire Book Company's most popular titles and has become an international bestseller.

Over 1 million copies sold!
The Simple Truths Presented in This Book Are
the Basis of All Success.

DYNAMIC THINKING

Techniques of Achieving
Self-Confidence and Success

by Melvin Powers

Dynamic Thinking will teach you what these truths are and will provide effective techniques for putting them to work in your life. You will learn how to harness the power of your conscious and subconscious minds and use that power to accomplish whatever you want!

Although these techniques are quite simple, they have proven themselves time and again. Those who are using them are well on the road to success, or have already achieved their goals. What others have done, you can do! It is never too late to succeed.

You need only use these techniques for a short period of time to experience a dramatic change in your mental outlook. You will be inspired. Your way of thinking and your way of life will change. Your inner strength and self-confidence will increase. Your enthusiasm and determination to succeed will skyrocket. Soon you will be able to achieve goals you never dreamed possible.

Melvin Powers' classic book *Dynamic Thinking* is your blueprint to dynamic living. It provides you with an opportunity to build the life you've wanted but never dared to believe you could have.